Learning to Program Java

Learning to Program Java

Edward Hill, Jr.

iUniverse, Inc.
New York Lincoln Shanghai

Learning to Program Java

Copyright © 2005 by Edward Hill, Jr.

All rights reserved. No part of this book may be used or reproduced by any means, graphic, electronic, or mechanical, including photocopying, recording, taping or by any information storage retrieval system without the written permission of the publisher except in the case of brief quotations embodied in critical articles and reviews.

iUniverse books may be ordered through booksellers or by contacting:

iUniverse
2021 Pine Lake Road, Suite 100
Lincoln, NE 68512
www.iuniverse.com
1-800-Authors (1-800-288-4677)

ISBN-13: 978-0-595-35422-1 (pbk)
ISBN-13: 978-0-595-79917-6 (ebk)
ISBN-10: 0-595-35422-X (pbk)
ISBN-10: 0-595-79917-5 (ebk)

Printed in the United States of America

Contents

Preface xi

1. **Learning to Program Java an Introduction** 1
   1.1. A Simple Java Model Program 1
   1.2. Simple Java Console Input and Output 5
   1.3. Assignment Statement 6
   1.4. Arithmetic Operators 7
   1.5. Simple Control Statements 10
      1.5.1. if Statements 10
      1.5.2. for Statement 11
      1.5.3. while Statement 12
   1.6. Exercises 13

2. **Building Java Elements** 17
   2.1. Identifiers 17
      2.1.1. Reserved Words 18
   2.2. Variables 18
      2.2.1. Declaring Variables 18
      2.2.2. Assignment Statements 19
      2.2.3. Declaring and Initializing in One Step 19
   2.3. Constants 19
   2.4. Numerical Data Types 20
   2.5. Numeric Literals 20
   2.6. Shortcut Operators 21
   2.7. Numeric Type Conversion 21
   2.8. Character Data Type 22
   2.9. Boolean Data Type 23
   2.10. Operator Precedence 23
   2.11. Program Comments 24
   2.12. Exercises 25

v

3.	**Control Structures** 29
	3.1. Using if Statements 29
	3.1.1. The Simple if Statement 29
	3.1.2. The if else Statement 36
	3.1.3. Shortcut if Statements 42
	3.2. Using switch Statements 42
	3.3. Using Loop Structures 48
	3.3.1. The for Loop 48
	3.3.2. The while Loop 56
	3.3.3. The do Loop 64
	3.4. Using the Keywords break and continue 72
	3.5. Exercises 73
4.	**Methods** 77
	4.1. Introduction 77
	4.2. Creating a Method 77
	4.3. Calling a Method 80
	4.3.1. Passing Parameters 80
	4.3.2. Pass by Value 80
	4.4. Overloading Methods 81
	4.5. Creating Methods in Separate Classes 82
	4.6. Method Abstraction 83
	4.7. Recursion 85
	4.8. Recursion versus Iteration 86
	4.9. Exercises 87
5.	**Exception Handling** 89
	5.1. Introduction 89
	5.2. Exceptions and Exception Types 89
	5.3. Understanding Exception Handling 90
	5.3.1. Claiming Exceptions 91
	5.3.2. Throwing Exceptions 91
	5.3.3. Trying and Catching Exceptions 92
	5.4. Exercises 93

6.	**File Input and Output**	95
	6.1. Introduction	95
	6.2. File Classes	96
	6.3. File and Dialog Objects	96
	6.4. Keyboard Input	97
	6.5. File Input	100
	6.6. File Output	105
	6.7. Exercises	109
7.	**Object-Oriented Programming**	111
	7.1. Introduction	111
	7.2. Objects and Classes	112
	7.2.1. Declaring and Creating Objects	113
	7.2.2. Constructors	114
	7.2.3. Modifiers	115
	7.3. Passing Objects to Methods	116
	7.4. Instance Variables and Class Variables	116
	7.5. Instance Methods and Class Methods	117
	7.6. The Scope of Variables	117
	7.7. Packages	117
	7.7.1. Putting Classes into Packages	120
	7.7.2. Using Packages	120
	7.8. Exercises	121
8.	**Arrays and String**	123
	8.1. Introduction	123
	8.2. Declaring and Creating Arrays	124
	8.3. Initializing and Processing Arrays	125
	8.4. Array of Objects	125
	8.5. Copying Arrays	126
	8.6. Multidimensional Arrays	126
	8.7. The String Class	128
	8.7.1. String Comparisons	129
	8.7.2. String Concatenation	129
	8.7.3. Substrings	130
	8.7.4. String Length and Retrieving Individual Characters in a String	130

8.8. The StringBuffer Class 130
8.9. The StringTokenizer Class 131
8.10. Command-Line Arguments 132
    8.10.1. Passing Arguments to Java Programs 132
    8.10.2. Processing Command-Line Parameters 132
8.11. Exercises 133

9. Class Inheritance 137
9.1. Introduction 137
9.2. Superclasses and Subclasses 138
9.3. Calling Superclass Constructors 139
    9.3.1. Calling Superclass Methods 139
9.4. The Object class 140
9.5. The final and abstract Modifiers 140
9.6. Casting Objects 141
9.7. Processing Numeric Values as Objects 141
9.8. The Numeric Class 141
    9.8.1. Numeric Wrapper Class Constructors 142
    9.8.2. Numeric Class Constants 142
    9.8.3. Conversion Methods 142
    9.8.4. The valueOf ( ) and parseInt ( ) Methods 142
9.9. Exercises 143

10. Basic Graphical User Interface Components 145
10.1. Introduction 145
10.2. The Applet Class 146
    10.2.1. The init ( ) Method 148
    10.2.2. The start ( ) Method 148
    10.2.3. The paint ( ) Method 148
    10.2.4. The stop ( ) Method 148
    10.2.5. The destroy ( ) Method 148
    10.2.6. Example Applet and <applet> HTML Tag 148
    10.2.7. Applets with User Input and Output with GUI 150
    10.2.8. Running a Program as an Applet 156
10.3. Swing Overview 156
10.4. JOptionPane 157
10.5. JLabel 165

10.6. Event Handling Model	168
10.7. How Event Handling Works	169
10.8. JTextField and JPasswordField	170
10.9. JButton	176
10.10. JCheckBox	180
10.11. JComboBox	185
10.12. Mouse Event Handling	190
10.13. Keyboard Event Handling	198
10.14. Layout Managers	201
10.14.1. FlowLayout	202
10.14.2. BorderLayout	205
10.14.3. GridLayout	207
10.15. Panels	208
10.16. Exercises	211
11. Multithreading	**213**
11.1. Introduction	213
11.2. The Thread Class	214
11.3. The Runnable Interface	219
11.4. Synchronization	224
11.5. Exercises	225
About the Author	227
Index	229

Preface

Use as a Textbook

The design and analysis of efficient programs has been recognized as a key subject in computing. The study of programming machines is part of the core curriculum in computer science and computer engineering. Typically, in programs based upon semesters, Java computer programming is introduced in the first programming course. In some computer science curriculums in the first semester Java programming is introduced with laboratory work. This is followed by a second semester programming course in Java that emphasizes many of the advance features in the language. After two semesters of programming Java the students are introduced to their first semester course in data structures and other computer science courses. This "Learning to Program Java" text book is designed as the first course of a two semester course in Java programming. Selected topics from the Java programming language are introduced to facilitate a beginner programming in Java. All exercises are programming problems. Programming problems are used as exercises to enforce a programming paradigm. A high percent of learning to program is highly correlated with the practice of designing and implementing programs for specific requirements. The translator or compiler will enhance the student knowledge through the trail and error process of removing errors from their programs. Emphasis is on defining Java constructs and their use in programming. Students are encouraged to program all the exercises at the end of each Chapter. Also students are encouraged to program their own applications to enhance their knowledge base. The idea is to program as many applications as possible using various Java constructs to improve programming skills in the Java programming language. Emphasis is placed on programming applications requirements. To enforce this paradigm Chapters are organized to maximize the learning process. Chapters on Exceptions and File Input and Output are introduced early in the text. After the file input and output are introduced all programs should read and write files to devices to maximize the learning experience. These topics are not treated for completeness. For example the

Arrays and String chapter implements the fundamentals of array processing and does not cover topics on vectors.

Prerequisites

This book is written assuming that the reader comes to it with certain knowledge. It is assumed that the reader is familiar with algebra. The reader understands that the text is designed for students willing to program Java, including:

- Variables and expressions
- Methods
- Decision structures (such as if-statements, and switch-statements)
- Iteration structures (for-loops and while-loops)
- File input and output
- Class definition and use
- Object definition and use
- Package definition and use
- Event definition and use
- Graphic User Interface definition and use
- Thread definition and use.

For the Instructor

This book is intended primarily as a textbook for a first semester Java Programming course in which the students have no object programming language skills.

1

Learning to Program Java an Introduction

1.1. A Simple Java Model Program

A simple Java model program consists of three parts. Part one of a Java program is the head. The head of a Java program defines the class name which is always the name of the file in which the program is stored with an extension of **.java**. The class name is followed by an open block and the class ends with a close class block. A block is opened with a curly left bracket "{"and closed with a curly right bracket"}."

```
public class myfirst {
```

The class name is **myfirst** and the class file name is always the class name, in this case it is **myfirst.java**.

The second part of a java program is a set of class declaration variables and methods that define the meaning of the class. **Methods** are well defined program units. Methods are detailed in the Chapter on Methods. A special method must be defined in every Java program. The special method is **public static void main (String Arg [ ]) {   }.**

Java is an object programming language with several primitive declaration types. Some primitive declaration types are **int** for integer, **float** or **double** for floating point or real, **boolean** for Boolean, and **char** for character. String is a special type and will be discussed in the Arrays and String chapter. Public declarations are available in methods that are defined in other methods. In other words, variables declared in one method may be accessed in other methods. The third part is the class tail indicated by a right curly bracket "}."

Implement a simple Java program that initializes a variable call trucks to an amount of gravel and a variable car to an amount of sand. Read the total number of trucks and cars from the keyboard and print the results on the console. Detail steps to implement the Java program are:

1. Define the Java class head myfirst that include imported packages and variable declarations. Java packages are discussed in Chapter 7.

    ```
    import java.io.*;
    public class myfirst      /* Class Head */
    { // Global variables defined in the head of the class block
      private static int sand;
      // Assign class variables values
      private static int gravel = 30;
    ```

2. You plan to read from the key board. Define a Java reader to manage input from the keyboard to your Java program. BufferedReader is discussed in Chapter 6.

    ```
    // Create a single shared BufferedReader for keyboard input.
    private static BufferedReader stdin = new BufferedReader (new InputStreamReader(System.in));
    ```

3. Define the head of the unique main Java method with variable declarations. The throws IOException statement is discussed in Chapter 5.

    ```
    // The main Java Method
    public static void main (String arg [ ])
       throws IOException
    { // Local variables defined in the head of the main method block
      int truck;
      int car;
      int number;
    ```

4. Initialize a class variable and write assignment statements to calculate gravel for the variable **truck** and sand for the variable **car**.

    ```
    // Assign a value to the class variable sand
    sand = 10;
    // Assignments for arithmetic statements
    truck = gravel + gravel;
    car = sand + sand;
    ```

5. Input the number of cars and trucks using the BufferedReader class for keyboard input. The input is a string stored in a variable called **input**.

    ```
    System.out.println("My First Java Program");
    System.out.println(" ");
    // Input the number of cars and trucks
    System.out.println ("Type the number of cars and trucks and
                        press enter ");
    String input = stdin.readLine ( );
    ```

6. Convert the String received from the keyboard to an integer. Store the integer in a variable called **number**.

    ```
    // Convert input to an integer
    number = Integer.parseInt (input);
    ```

7. Print the results on the console. Call a Java system program to exit your program that reclaims the Java program resources.

    ```
    // Print the number of cars and trucks
    System.out.println ("Number of cars and trucks = "+number);
    //Print output on the console
    System.out.println ("Trucks carry gravel. The amount is " +
                        truck);
    System.out.println ("Cars carry sand. The amount is " + car);
    System.exit (0);
    ```

8. Define the tail of the Java main method.

   ```
   } // End of Java main method
   ```

9. Define the tail of the Java class myfirst.

   ```
   } // Class tail or end of Java class myfirst
   ```

The terms Exceptions and BufferedReader are detailed in Chapters 5 and 6. A simple Java program saved with a name **myfirst.java** is detailed in Figure 1.

```
import java.io.*;
public class myfirst       /* Class Head */
{ // Global variables defined in the head of the class block
  private static int sand;
  // Assign a value to a class variable
  private static int gravel = 30;

  // -----------------------
  // Other Java methods
  // -----------------------

  // Unique main Java method

  // Create a single shared BufferedReader for keyboard input
  private static BufferedReader stdin = new BufferedReader (new
  InputStreamReader (System.in));

  // The main Java Method
  public static void main (String arg [ ])
    throws IOException
  { // Local variables defined in the head of the main method block
    int truck;
    int car;
    int number;

    // Assign a value to a class variable
    sand = 10;
    // Assignments for arithmetic statements
    truck = gravel + gravel;
    car = sand + sand;
```

```
        System.out.println ("My First Java Program");
        System.out.println (" ");
        // Input the number of cars and trucks
        System.out.println ("Type the number of cars and trucks and
                            press enter");
        String input = stdin.readLine ();
        // Convert input to an integer
        number = Integer.parseInt (input);

        //Print the number of cars and trucks
        System.out.println ("Number of cars and trucks = "+number);
        // Print output on the console
        System.out.println ("Trucks carry gravel. The amount is " +
                            truck);
        System.out.println ("Cars carry sand. The amount is " + car);
        System.exit (0);
    } // End of Java main method
} // Class tail or end of Java class myfirst
```

Figure I. A Simple Java Program

The first Java program execution results for a total of 45 trucks and cars are:

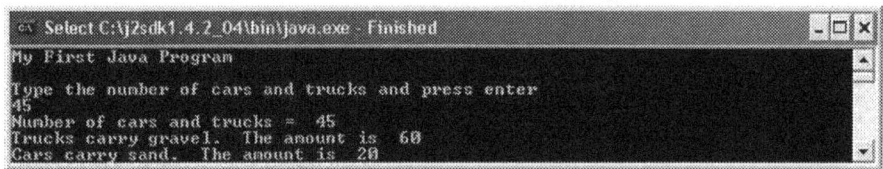

1.2. Simple Java Console Input and Output

Variables used in Java input statements must be defined and allocated. Variables are defined or allocated using declaration statements. Define or allocate variables **sand** and **gravel** as integer variables.

```
    int sand;
    int gravel;
```

Another form of the integer declaration is int sand, gravel;
Simple Java input from the console is
System.in.readln (sand, gravel); or System.in.readln (sand); System.in.readln (gravel);
Simple Java output to the console is
System.out.println ("The amount of sand is " + sand);
System.out.println ("This is gravel for the yellow brick road. The amount is " + gravel);
Input and output statements are detailed in Figure 1. Java input, output, and control characters are detailed in the Chapter on File Input and Output.

1.3. Assignment Statement

A variable is something that changes. High level languages provide rules or constructs that allow users to define variables. A **variable** is a set of alphabets and digits of which the first is an alphabet connected by spaces or underscores whose length is less than 255 characters. Variables are allocated by associating each variable with a physical memory location in the computer memory. Values are stored in variables with an assignment operator. The assignment operator involves a left member and a right member that defines an assignment statement. In the Java programming language the assignment operator is "=." The operation is defined as a destructive operation in which the content of the right member address is stored in the left member address. For example V = N; implies that the content of the memory address, the right member allocated to N is stored in the address of the left member allocated to V. The previous content of the address allocated to V is destroyed and replaced by the content of the address allocated to N. The assignment operator is detailed in Figure 2.

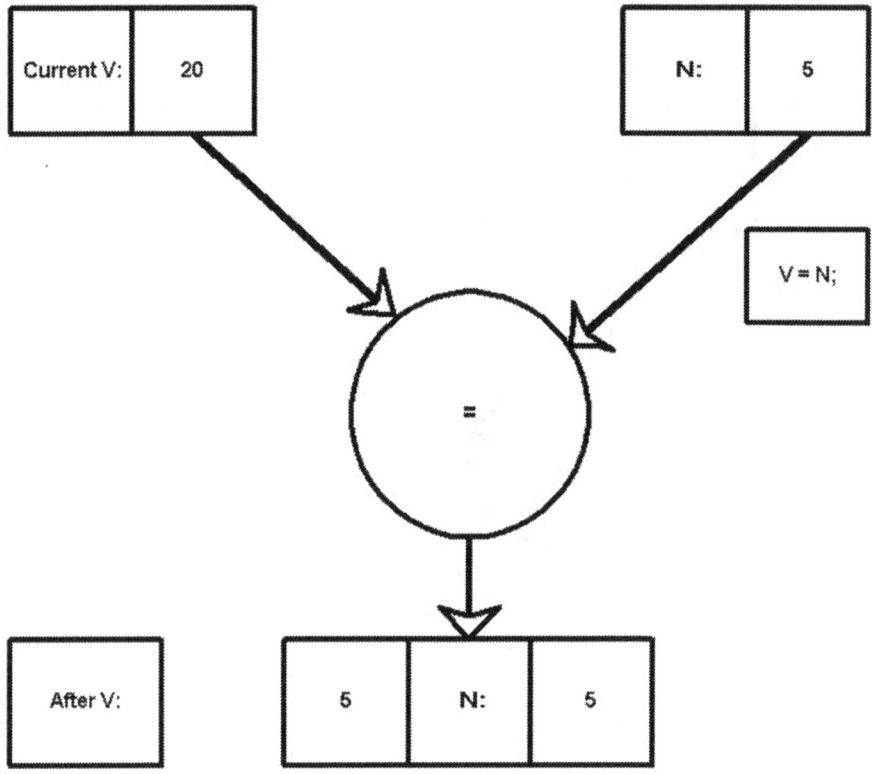

Figure 2. Assignment Statement Action

1.4. Arithmetic Operators

Basic arithmetic operators in the Java programming language are addition "+", subtraction "-", division "/", and multiplication "*." The precedence of these operators is the same as those learned in elementary arithmetic.

Addition Operator "+"

Definition of "+" is add a constant number or the content or a variable and store the sum in a variable. For example, V = V + N; is defined as add the content of the memory address assigned to V to the contents of the memory address assigned to N and store the results in the address assigned to V. The sum is stored in V destroying the previous content in the address assigned to V. An addition operation is detailed in Figure 3.

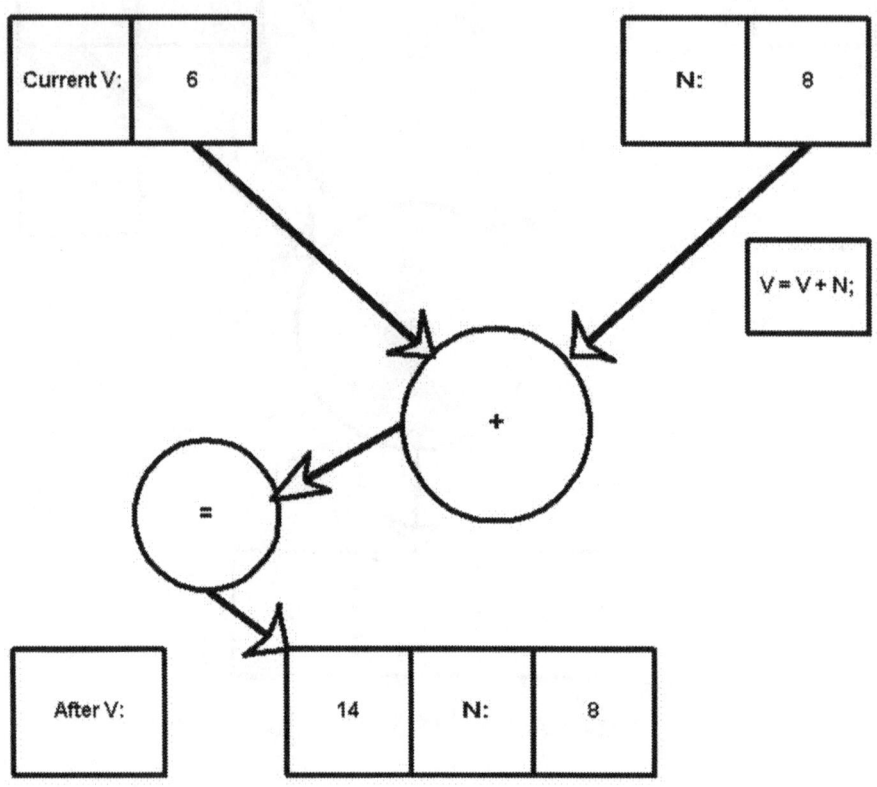

Figure 3. Addition Arithmetic Operation

Other operators "-, *, and /" are replaced in the process and computed with results stored in the same manner as the "+" operator. An expression example is detailed in Figure 4.

X = Z + Q * L;

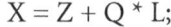

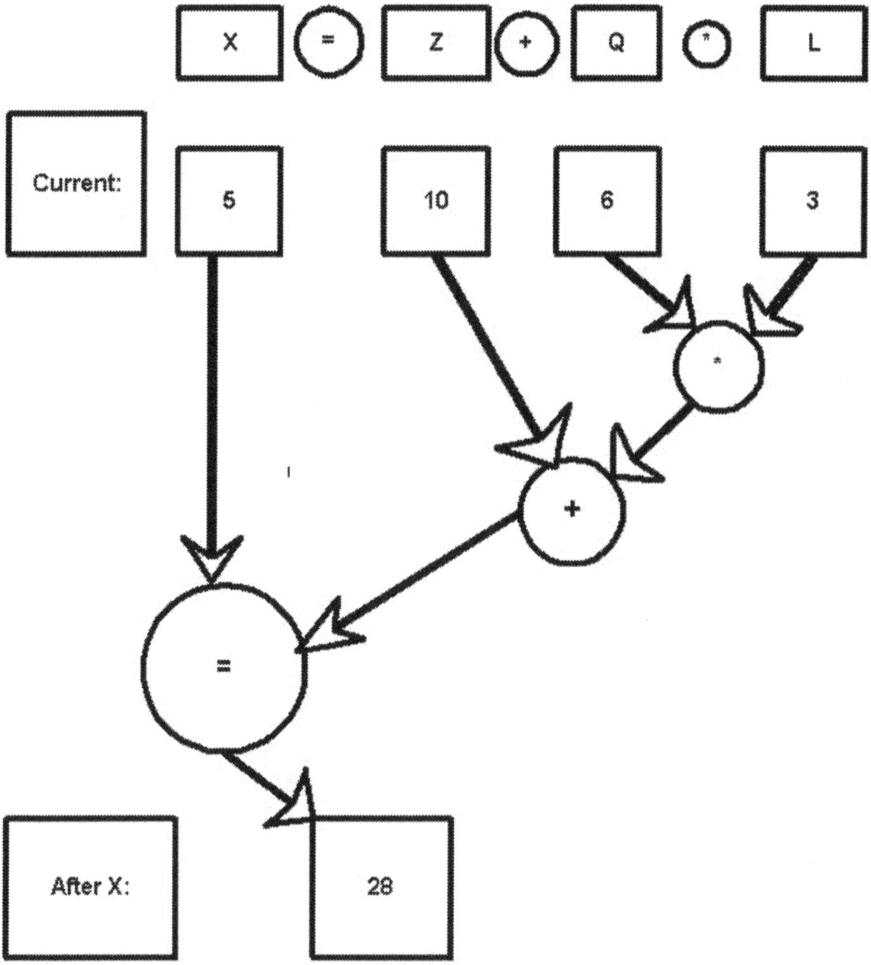

Figure 4. Assignment Statement with an Expression

1.5. Simple Control Statements

Control statements are used to execute program segments as a function of a relation operator. In many cases expressions are evaluated and action is taken based on the relational operators ==, <, <, <=, >=, !=, OR ||, AND &&, and NOT!. A comparison is made and an indicator is set. Code is generated by the high level language translator to test the machine indicator to carry out the meaning of the control statement. There are many control statements in Java. Three control statements in Java are if, for, and while. Java control statements are detailed in the Chapter on Control Structures.

1.5.1. if Statements

The syntax of a simple form of the if statement is

```
if (expression relational operator expression) | Boolean expression)
    statement;
| { // open code block
    statement; statement; … } // close code block
[Option Open]
  else
    statement;
    | { statement; statement; … }
[Option Close]
```

The meta-symbol | means OR.

Code segments with an if statement

```
int a, b, c, d;
a = 5;
b = 20;
c = 40;
d = -78;
if ((d + c / 4) <= (b - d))
    a = b + c;
  else
    { c = a - d;
      b = c * a;
    }
```

Code segment with a logical operation

```
int a = 5;
int b = 20;
int c = 40;
int d = -78;
boolean x, y;
x = True;
y = false;
if (x)
   c = a - d;
   else
     if (x && y)
        { a = b + c * d;
          b = a;
        }
```

1.5.2. for Statement

Programming languages offer users the ability to repeat the execution of code segments with a count control. This statement starts by initializing a loop control variable to an initial value. The translator generates code to test the control variable against a loop bound. If the test is invalid the scope of the loop is skipped and the next statement after the loop scope is executed; otherwise the control variable is incremented or decremented and the scope of the loop is executed. The **scope of the loop** is the set of statements in the block defined by the for-statement.

The syntax of a for statement is

```
for (control variable = initial value; control variable relation
operator control bound; control variable increment or decrement)
statement; | { statement; statement; ... }
```

The meta-symbol | means OR.

A simple code segment is

```
int j;
int a = 5;
int b = 20;
int c = 40;
int d = -78;
```

```
boolean x, y;
x = True;
y = false;
for (j = a; j <= c; j = j + 1)
   { b = j * c;
      d = b + a;
   }
```

1.5.3. while Statement

The while statement is another loop control statement in Java controlled with a sentinel variable. There are many loop control statements in the Java programming language.

The syntax of a while statement is

```
while (control variable | expression relation operator control
variable | expression) statement; | { statement; statement; …
statement; }
```

A code segment with a while statement is

```
int j = 0;
int a = 5;
int b = 20;
int c = 40;
int d = -78;
while (j <= 6)
   { b = j * c;
      d = b + a;
      j = j + 1;
   }
```

This loop will execute and increment j by one on each iteration until the condition j <= 6 is violated. In this while loop the variable j is called the sentential variable.

1.6. Exercises

Implement Java programs for all exercises. Insert the program segments in the Java main method in Figure 1. Translate the Java program at the command prompt with

    javac myfirst.java.

If your operating system is not configured for Java make the directory that contains the Java source code to be compiled the current directory. Use a path to the installed Java directory and add the subdirectory **bin** to the path. The **bin** subdirectory contains **javac.exe**. For example, assume that Java is installed on the root of a logical c-drive in a directory call **myjava** and you want to compile **myfirst.java** that is stored in a directory in the root of the c-drive called **mytest**. A command to compile **myfirst.java** is

    c:\myjava\bin\javac c:\mytest\myfirst.java

This command produces byte code in a file called **myfirst.class**. Execute the byte code at the command prompt with

    java myfirst.

If your operating system is not configured for Java make the directory that contains the Java compiled code the current directory. Use a path to the installed Java directory and add the subdirectory **bin** to the path. The **bin** subdirectory contains **java.exe**. For example, assume that Java is installed on the root of a logical c-drive in a directory call **myjava** and you want to execute **myfirst.class** that is stored in a directory in the root of the c-drive called **mytest**. A command to execute **myfirst.class** is

    c:\myjava\bin\java c:\mytest\myfirst

This is your moment of truth. Complete each exercise to improve your chances of success in other chapters.

1. Declare or define integer variables for the vowels in the alphabet. Set each variable to a number that is a multiple of 21. Print the variable content to the console.

2. Declare or define 10 floating-point variables of length 3 in which the first letter is a letter from the alphabet. The second and third character in the variable should be another letter from the alphabet or a digit from 0 to 9. Do

not use spaces in the variable definitions. Assign a number to each variable between 2 and 300. Print the variable content to the console. Write at least 10 expressions using three arithmetic operations to calculate and assign the result to one of the variables. Print each calculated result to the console.

3. Declare or define variables X, Y, A, B, C as integers and initialize the variables to zero. Print the content of the variables on the console. Assign to X, A, B, and C values 23, 3, 2, 106 respectively. Print X, A, B, and C on the counsel. Calculate the quadratic function using the value of X with coefficients A, B, and C, store the result in Y. Print Y on the console.

4. Declare two integer variables and two floating-point variables of your choice to calculate the perimeter of an object. Assign values to the variables and calculate the perimeter of an object. Print the perimeter on the console.

5. Write an application that reads four integers and prints their average.

6. Write an application that reads three floating point numbers and prints their sum, difference, and product.

7. Write an application to read a Fahrenheit temperature number from the user. Convert the number read to Celsius and print the result.

8. Write an application that converts miles to feet. Read the miles value from the user as a floating point value. Print the converted result.

9. Write an application that reads values representing time duration in hours, minutes, and seconds, and then print the equivalent total number of seconds.

10. Write an application that reads the radius of a sphere and print its volume.

    volume = (¾) * 3.14 * (radius)^3

11. Write an application that computes the number of miles per gallon of gas for a trip. Accept as input a floating point number that represents the total gas used. Also accept two integers representing the odometer readings at the start and end of the trip. Compute the number of kilometers per liter and print the result.

    one mile = 1.60935 kilometers

12. Write an application that reads in the length and width of a rectangular yard in feet and the length and width of a rectangular house in meters placed in the yard. Compute the time required to cut the lawn around the house. Assume the mowing rate in square meters per minutes is read as an input item.

2
Building Java Elements

Basic Java programming is part of the programming language repository. This is a part of the basic programming language experience that resulted from programming all the exercises in Chapter 1. If the basic programming skills are not at your approved level search other books for programming problems that cover the introduction content. It is advised to program applied physical problems using the basic Java statements until your level of knowledge is suitable to advance to Java language elements.

2.1. Identifiers

Programmers use symbols to refer to things in Java programs. The Java programming language uses a set of special symbols to define identifiers. These **identifiers** are used for variables, constants, methods, classes, and packages. The rules for naming identifiers are:
- The first character is a letter, an underscore, or a dollar sign.
- Identifiers cannot contain operators.
- Identifiers cannot contain reserved words.
- Identifiers cannot be true, false, or null.
- Identifiers can be of any length less than or equal to 255 characters.

Java uses the Unicode specification for characters. The characters represent letters in international languages. Descriptive identifiers aid in program readability and maintenance. Java is case sensitive.

2.1.1. Reserved Words

Java programming language **reserved words** are words used by the compiler implementer that cannot be used in programmer identifiers. Java reserved words are detailed in Figure 5.

abstract	finally	protected
bolean	float	public
break	for	return
byte	goto	short
case	if	static
char	implements	super
class	import	switch
const	instanceof	synchronized
continue	int	this
default	interface	throw
do	long	transient
double	native	try
else	new	void
extends	package	volatile
final	private	while

Figure 5. Java Reserved Words

2.2. Variables

Variables are used to store data. Storing of datum in a variable is detailed in Figure 2.

2.2.1. Declaring Variables

Variables are used to represent different types of data. Variables must be declared before they are used. **Declarations** are defined with a data type and a valid variable. The syntax of a variable declaration is

```
datatype variablename;
```

Examples of variable declarations are:

```
int q;      // declares q to be an integer variable;
char h;     // declares h to be a character variable;
```

2.2.2. Assignment Statements

A declared variable is used to store a value. A value is stored into a variable using an assignment statement. The syntax of an assignment statement is

```
variable = value;
```

Examples of assignment statements are:

```
q = 45;     // assign 45 to q;
h = 'E';    // assign 'E' to h;
```

Assignment statement actions are detailed in Figure 2 of Section 1.3.

2.2.3. Declaring and Initializing in One Step

Variables may be declared and initialized to a value in one step.

Example of declaring a variable and initializing it to a value

```
int q = 45;
```

This is equivalent to

```
int q;
q = 45;
```

A variable must be declared and assigned an initial value before it can be read.

2.3. Constants

A **constant variable** or **constant** is a variable whose value never changes. Constants are useful defining shared values for methods of an object. Constants are used for giving meaningful names to object wide values that will never change. In Java, you can create constants only for instance or class variables.

A constant is declared by using the **final** keyword before the variable declaration and including an initial value for the variable.

Examples of constants are:

```
final boolean test = false;
final int minimum = 600;
final float pi = 3.141;
```

2.4. Numerical Data Types

The Java numeric data types are byte, short, int, long, float, and double. The data types **byte, short, int,** and **long** are for integers, and the data types float and double are for real numbers. All data types are reserved words. A list of reserved words is detailed in Figure 3. Java numerical data types and their precisions are detailed in Figure 6.

Data Type	Content	Default Values	Minimum Value	Maximum Value
byte	Integer	0	-128	127
short	Integer	0	-32768	32767
int	Integer	0	-2147483648	2147483647
long	Integer	0	-9223372036854775808	9223372036854775807
float	Real	0.0	1.40129846432481707e-45	3.40282346638528860e+38
double	Real	0.0	4.94065645841246544e-324d	1.79769313486231570e+308d

Figure 6. Java Numerical Data Types and Their Precisions

2.5. Numeric Literals

A **literal** is a constant that appears directly in a program. Examples of literals are:

```
final double one_side = 96.0;
double product = 4.0 * one_side + 6;
```

The literal constants are 96.0, 4.0, and 6. The data type constant for 6 is set to int by default. The constant for 6 is set to a **long** by appending l or L.

```
double product = 4.0 * one_side + 6L;
```

Integers can be expressed as octal or hexadecimal. A leading 0 indicates that a number is octal, for example 0005. A leading 0x or 0X means that it is in hex, for example 0xFF. Hexadecimal numbers can contain regular digits (0–9) or upper or lowercase hex digits (a–f or A–F).

2.6. Shortcut Operators

Programmers are interested in writing language statement to combine more than one operation in a single language statement. These operations should be used by programmers that understand each single statement that results in the combine operation. For example the single statement to increment a declared variable j by 24 is

```
j = j + 24;
```

This statement is equivalent to

```
j += 24;
```

The operator += is called a shortcut operator. The meaning of this shortcut operator is defined to operate from left to right on the operator. A number 24 is added to the current content of j and the result is stored in the address assigned to j.

Other Java shortcut operators that operate from left to right are -=, *=, /=, and %=. A shortcut operator that increments a declared variable m by 1 may precede the variable or follow the variable as ++m or m++. Use --m or m-- to decrement m. That is to say, ++m and m++ are the same as m = m + 1. The decrement statement --m and m-- are the same as m = m - 1;

2.7. Numeric Type Conversion

Programmers have needs to calculate expressions with mixed data types. Java is a strong typed language. The programmer must perform type conversions to assign the result to a variable. The method of converting from one data type to another is called **type casting**. Type casting in Java is accomplished by preceding the variable to be converted with the new data type enclosed in parentheses. Type casting is detailed in a code segment as

```
int small_cars = 50;
float large_cars = 120.50;
float all_cars = 0.0;
all_cars = (float)small_cars + large_cars;
```

The last statement in the code segment is made by type casting the int small_cars to float small_cars to be added to **large_cars** and assigned to float all_cars.

2.8. Character Data Type

The character data type, char, is used to declare a single character.

```
char check;
```

A character literal is expressed by a single character surrounded by single quotes.

```
check = 'T';
```

Characters are stored as 16-bit Unicode characters. A set of special non printable characters used as escape codes are detailed in Figure 7.

Escape	Meaning
\n	Newline
\t	Tab
\b	Backspace
\r	Carriage return
\f	Formfeed
\\	Backslash
\'	Single quote
\"	Double quote
\ddd	Octal
\xdd	Hexadecimal
\udddd	Unicode character

The letters d in the octal, hex, and Unicode escapes represents a positive number or a hexadecimal digit (**a–f or A–F**).

Figure 7. Character Escape Codes

2.9. Boolean Data Type

The domain of the boolean type consists of two values, true and false. For example, assign a boolean value of true to a boolean variable **left_turn**.

```
boolean left_turn = true;
```

The two types of operators associated with Boolean values are comparison and Boolean. Comparison operators for Boolean values are detailed in Figure 8.

Operator	Name	Example	Answer
<	less than	8 < 10	true
<=	less than or equal to	8 <= 10	true
>	greater than	8 > 10	false
>=	greater than or equal to	8 >= 10	false
==	equal to	8 == 10	false
!=	not equal to	8 != 10	true

Figure 8. Comparison Operators for Boolean Values

Boolean operators for Boolean values are detailed in Figure 9.

Operator	Name	Description
!	not	logical negation
&&	and	logical conjunction
||	or	logical disjunction
^	exclusive or	logical exclusion

Figure 9. Boolean Operators for Boolean values

2.10. Operator Precedence

In order to perform an evaluation of an expression an order must be defined on the operators in the programming language. Java implements an order on the operators called an operator precedence that ensures that expressions are correctly evaluated. When evaluating Java expressions the order of evaluation is from highest precedence to lowest precedence. Java operator precedence is detailed in Figure 10. Precedence in Figure 10 with the lowest number is the highest precedence.

Precedence	Operator
First	++, --
Second	*, /, %
Third	+, -
Fourth	<, <=, >, =>
Fifth	==, !=
Sixth	&&
Seventh	||
Eighth	=, +=, -=, +=, /=, %=

Figure 10. Java Operator Precedence

2.11. Program Comments

Java offers two types of comments. One comment is the //. Any line of code with a // is a comment for all characters to the end of line. The second comment type allows users to comment blocks of text. The start of this comment is a comment head /*. After the comment head follows any number of lines of text. The comment ends with a comment tail */. An example of the first type of comment is,

```
boolean right_hand = false; // right_hand is defined as a boolean
                               variable.
```

For example, the second comment form is

```
/* number_of is defined as an integer variable and initialized to
a value of 50 */
int number_of = 50;
```

Notice that the second comment spanned more that one line. However, this type of comment may be used on a single line.

Program comments are important in a programming enterprise. In many organizations standards are defined to ensure well defined comments in programs. For example, any variable used in a program must be a word that exists in a standard dictionary.

2.12. Exercises

1. Write an application that reads four numbers, representing the number of quarters, dimes, nickels, and pennies the user possesses, and print the total number of dollars and cents.

2. Write an application to calculate the selling price of items at a discount store where

    Selling price = List price - Discount + Tax.

    Read List price, Discount, and Tax. Print the calculated Selling price.

3. Design and implement an application that reads an integer value and prints the sum of all even integers between 2 and the input value, inclusive. Print an error message if the input is less than 2. Stop reading numbers if the number read is negative.

4. Write an application that reads floating point variables x1, x2, x3, and x4. Calculate the slope of a line through the two points (x1, y1) and (x2, y2). Use the formula

    m = (y1 - y2) / (x1 - x2).

    Print the results with a message if m is positive and another message if the slope m is negative.

5. Write a complete Java program that prompts the user for the Cartesian coordinates of two points, (x_1, y_1) and (x_2, y_2), and display the distance between them computed by using the formula:

    distance = $((x_2 - x_1)^2 + (y_2 - y_1)^2)^{1/2}$

6. Write a Java program that read values from the keyboard into x and y and compute and display the absolute difference (e.g., if x is 12 and y is 22, the absolute difference is 10).

7. Write a program that reads two data items from the keyboard and compute their sum, difference, product, and quotient. Display the computation results.

8. Write a program that reads in the numerators and denominators of two fractions from the keyboard. The program should display the product of the two fractions as a fraction and as a percent.

9. Write a program that converts miles to kilometers. One mile equals 1.60935 kilometers. Read the miles value from the keyboard from the user as a floating point value.

10. Write a program that reads the radius of a sphere from the keyboard and display its volume and surface area. The formulas where r represents the radius are:

    Volume = (¾) * 3.14 * r^3

    Surface area = 4 * 3.14 * r^2

11. If you invest P dollars at R% interest rate compounded annually, in N years, your investment will grow to

    $P(1 - (R / 100)^{N+1}) / (1 - (R / 100))$

    dollars. Write an application that accepts P, R, and N from the keyboard and computes the amount of money earned after N years. Display your results.

12. Write an application that accepts a person's weight from the keyboard and displays the number of calories the person needs in one day. A person needs 19 calories per pound of body weight. The formula is

    calories = bodyweight * 19

13. A quantity called body mass index (BMI) is used to calculate the risk of weight-related health problems. BMI is computed as

    BMI = w / h_2, where w is weight in kilograms and h is height in meters.

    A BMI of about 20 to 25 is considered normal. Write an application that accepts weight and height as integers from the keyboard and display the BMI.

14. Write a program that contains variables that hold your tuition fee and book fee. Read your tuition fee and book fee from the keyboard and compute the sum of the variables. Display the sum of your tuition fee and book fee.

15. Write a program that calculates and displays the weekly salary for an employee who earns $25.50 an hour, works 40 regular hours and earns time and one-half for overtime hours worked. Overtime hours are the number of hours worked each week that exceed 40 hours. Read the number of hours worked each week from the keyboard. Calculate and display the weekly salary.

3

Control Structures

All the information in Chapter 1 and Chapter 2 is useful in writing Java programs. No mechanisms exist to execute program segments in a cyclic manner. No mechanisms exist to control program execution flow within program segments. In this chapter mechanisms are defined to execute program segments in a cyclic manner and control the execution flow within program segments.

3.1. Using if Statements

Java if statements are defined as a simple if or if else statements. The simple if statement executes a statement or program segment for a true if condition. A second form an if statement execute a statement or program segment based on whether the condition is true or false and the statement is defined as if else.

3.1.1. The Simple if Statement

The syntax for the simple if statement is

```
if (Boolean Expression or Comparison Operator Result)
    statement; or {statements}
```

The first line of if (Boolean Expression or Comparison Operator with Expression) is called **if head**. A statement or program segment defined by {statements} that follow if head is called **if body**. Figure 11 details if head and if body. A statement is any legal Java statement.

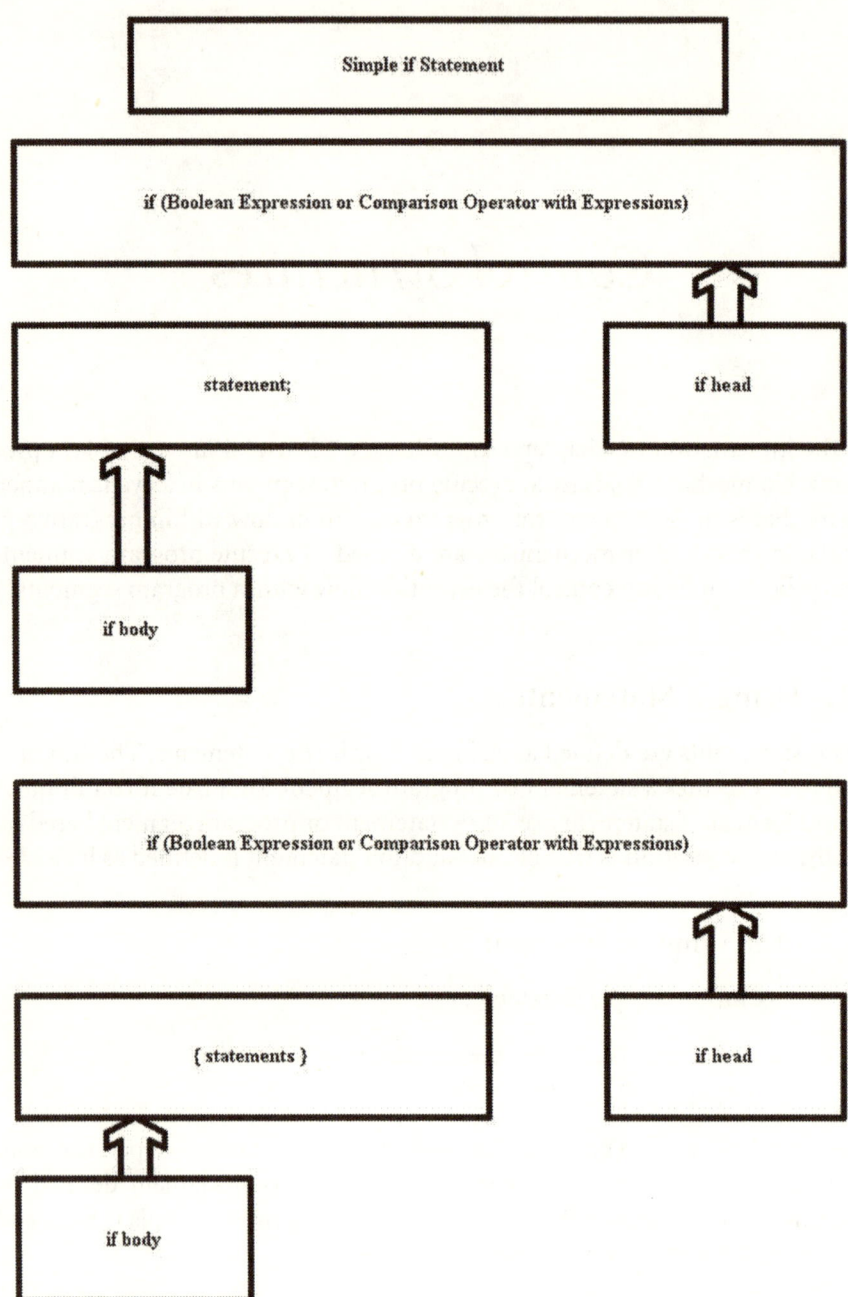

Figure 11. if Head and if Body

An evaluation of if head to true results in the execution of a single statement following if head or a program segment defined by {statements}. Otherwise, the next executable statement is executed. Figure 12 details the flow of a simple if statement.

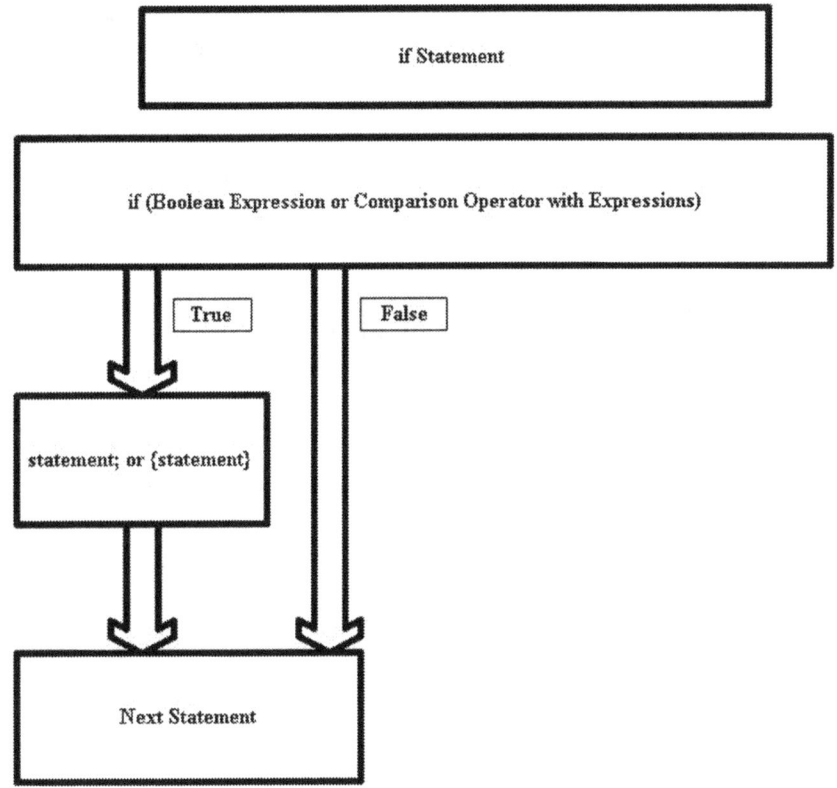

Figure 12. Simple if Statement Program Flow

For example, write an application to read from the concole six integers between 0 and 100. Use three integer variables to count the number of times the numbers read were in the ranges 0 to 25, 26 to 60, and 61 to 100. Sum the numbers read in each range. Exit the application when a negative integer is read.

Implementation of a select range steps are:

1. Implement a Java program that uses if-statements to select ranges call **ifrange**. Define the class head with an import package and variable declarations. Java packages are discussed in Chapter 7.

   ```
   import java.io.*;
   public class ifrange
   {
     // Define and initialize the count range variables
     private static int cnt0_25 = 0;
     private static int cnt26_60 = 0;
     private static int cnt61_100 = 0;
     // Define and initialize the sum range variables
     private static int sum0_25 = 0;
     private static int sum26_60 = 0;
     private static int sum61_100 = 0;
   ```

2. Define a Java Reader to input data from the keyboard. BufferedReader is discussed in Chapter 6.

   ```
   private static BufferedReader stdin = new BufferedReader
   (new InputStreamReader(System.in));
   ```

3. Define the head of the Java main method with variable declarations. The Java throws IOException statement is discussed in Chapter 5.

   ```
   public static void main (String arg [ ])
       throws IOException
   { // Define the input integer variable
     int intest = 0;
   ```

4. Use the Java Reader to read a number from the keyboard and store it in a variable called **input**. The number read is a string.

   ```
   System.out.println ("If Select");
   System.out.println (" ");
   System.out.println ("Enter a number between 0 and 100 and
                       press enter.");
   String input = stdin.readLine ( );
   ```

5. Convert the numbers read from the keyboard to an integer and store it in a variable called **intest**.

   ```
   intest = Integer.parseInt (input);
   ```

6. Write if-statements to select the range of the number read from the keyboard. Count the number of times the range was selected. Sum the number selected in a range.

```
// Test for the range 0 to 25.
if ((intest >= 0) && (intest <= 25))
  { // Increment the range counter.
    cnt0_25 = cnt0_25 + 1;
    // Add the new within range value to the range sum.
    sum0_25 = sum0_25 + intest;
    // Read another integer from the keyboard.
  }

// Test for the range 26 to 60.
if ((intest > 25) && (intest <= 60))
  { // Increment the range counter.
    cnt26_60 = cnt26_60 + 1;
    // Add the new within range value to the range sum.
    sum26_60 = sum26_60 + intest;
    // Read another integer from the keyboard.
  }

// Test for the range 61 to 100.
if ((intest > 60) && (intest <= 100))
  { // Increment the range counter.
    cnt61_100 = cnt61_100 + 1;
    // Add the new within range value to the range sum.
    sum61_100 = sum61_100 + intest;
    // Read another integer from the keyboard.
  }
```

7. When a negative number is read from the keyboard write the results of the selected range and sum of the numbers in the selected range on the console.

```
// Write program results.
if ((intest >= 0) && (intest <= 100))
    {
      System.out.println ("The count for range 0 to 25 is: " +
                          cnt0_25);
      System.out.println ("The sum for range 0 to 25 is: " +
                          sum0_25);
      System.out.println ("The count for range 26 to 60 is: " +
                          cnt26_60);
```

```
            System.out.println ("The sum for range 26 to 60 is: " +
                                sum26_60);
            System.out.println ("The count for range 61 to 100 is: " +
                                cnt61_100);
            System.out.println ("The sum for range 61 to 100 is: " +
                                sum61_100);
            System.exit (0);
         }
```

8. Define the tail of the Java main method.

   ```
   } // End main Method
   ```

9. Define the tail of the Java class ifrange.

   ```
   } // End class ifrange
   ```

Implemented application using if statements that is saved in a file called ifrange.java.

```
// ifrange
// An application that uses if statements to select ranges
// needed for BufferedReader, InputStreamReader, etc.
import java.io.*;
public class ifrange
{
  // Define and initialize the count range variables
  private static int cnt0_25 = 0;
  private static int cnt26_60 = 0;
  private static int cnt61_100 = 0;
  // Define and initialize the sum range variables
  private static int sum0_25 = 0;
  private static int sum26_60 = 0;
  private static int sum61_100 = 0;

  // Create a single shared BufferedReader for keyboard input
  private static BufferedReader stdin = new BufferedReader
  (new InputStreamReader (System.in));

  // The main Java Method
  public static void main (String arg [ ])
    throws IOException
  { // Define the input integer variable
    int intest = 0;
    System.out.println ("If Select");
```

```
System.out.println (" ");
// Read a string from the user.
System.out.println ("Enter a number between 0 and 100 and
                    press enter.");
String input = stdin.readLine ( );
// Convert input to an integer
intest = Integer.parseInt (input);

// Test for the range 0 to 25.
if ((intest >= 0) && (intest <= 25))
   { // Increment the range counter.
     cnt0_25 = cnt0_25 + 1;
     // Add the new within range value to the range sum.
     sum0_25 = sum0_25 + intest;
     // Read another integer from the keyboard.
   }

// Test for the range 26 to 60.
if ((intest > 25) && (intest <= 60))
   { // Increment the range counter.
     cnt26_60 = cnt26_60 + 1;
     // Add the new within range value to the range sum.
     sum26_60 = sum26_60 + intest;
     // Read another integer from the keyboard.
   }

// Test for the range 61 to 100.
if ((intest > 60) && (intest <= 100))
   { // Increment the range counter.
     cnt61_100 = cnt61_100 + 1;
     // Add the new within range value to the range sum.
     sum61_100 = sum61_100 + intest;
     // Read another integer from the keyboard.
   }

// Write program results.
if ((intest >= 0) && (intest <= 100))
   {
     System.out.println ("The count for range 0 to 25 is: " +
                         cnt0_25);
     System.out.println ("The sum for range 0 to 25 is: " +
                         sum0_25);
     System.out.println ("The count for range 26 to 60 is: " +
                         cnt26_60);
```

```
            System.out.println ("The sum for range 26 to 60 is: " +
                                sum26_60);
            System.out.println ("The count for range 61 to 100 is: " +
                                cnt61_100);
            System.out.println ("The sum for range 61 to 100 is: " +
                                sum61_100);
            System.exit (0);
        }
    } // End main Method
} // End class ifrange
```

A screen view of the ifrange class execution is:

```
C:\j2sdk1.4.2_04\bin\java.exe - Finished
If Select

Enter a number between 0 and 100 and press enter.
43
The count for range 0 to 25 is:   0
The sum for range 0 to 25 is:     0
The count for range 26 to 60 is:  1
The sum for range 26 to 60 is:    43
The count for range 61 to 100 is: 0
The sum for range 61 to 100 is:   0
```

3.1.2. The if else Statement

The simple if statement is executed if the specified condition is true. If the condition is false, nothing is done. In many cases, the programmer wants to take alternative actions when the condition is false. Alternative action is taken with if else statement. The syntax of if else is

```
if (Boolean Expression or Comparison Operator Result)
   statement; or {statements}
else
   statement; or {statements}
```

An evaluation of if head results in the execution of a single statement following if head or a program segment defined by {statement}. Else, if body after the else is executed with a single statement or a program segment defined by {statement}. Otherwise, the next executable statement based on if head evaluation is executed. Figure 13 details the flow of if else statement.

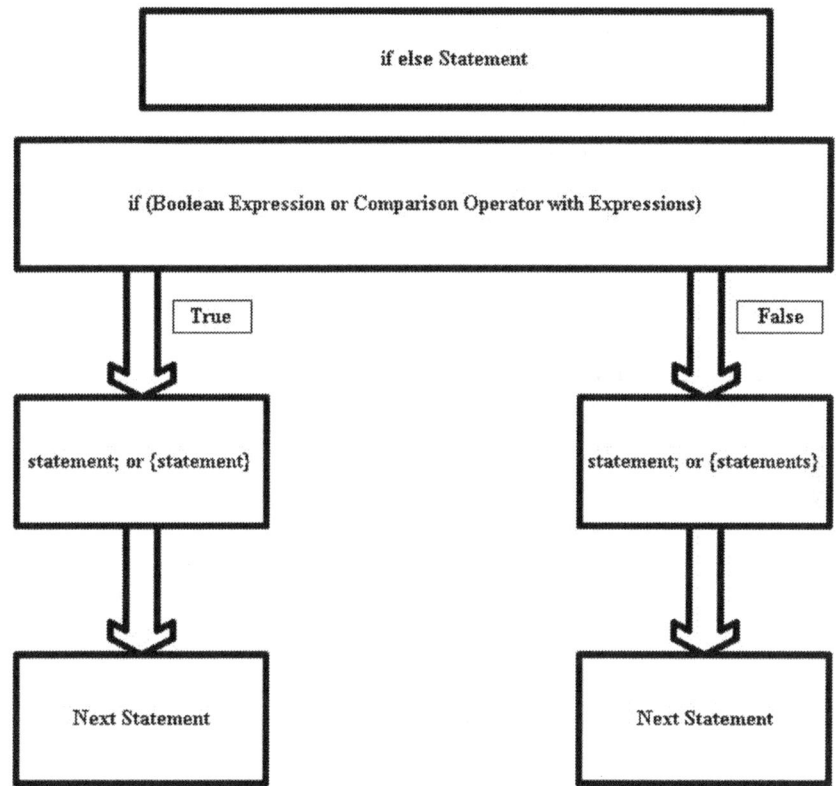

Figure 13. if else Statement Program Flow

For example, write an application to read from the counsel six integers between 0 and 100. Use three integer variables to count the number of times the numbers read were in the ranges 0 to 25, 26 to 60, and 61 to 100. Sum the numbers read in each range. Exit the application when a negative integer is read.

Implementation of a select range steps using if-else statements are:

1. Implement a Java program that uses if-else statements to select ranges call **elserang**. Define the class head with an import package and variable declarations. Java packages are discussed in Chapter 7.

```
import java.io.*;
public class elserang
{
  // Define and initialize the count range variables
  private static int cnt0_25 = 0;
  private static int cnt26_60 = 0;
  private static int cnt61_100 = 0;
  // Define and initialize the sum range variables
  private static int sum0_25 = 0;
  private static int sum26_60 = 0;
  private static int sum61_100 = 0;
```

2. Define a Java Reader to input data from the keyboard. Create a single shared BufferedReader for keyboard input. BufferedReader is discussed in Chapter 6.

```
private static BufferedReader stdin = new BufferedReader (new
InputStreamReader (System.in));
```

3. Define the head of the Java main method with variable declarations. The Java throws IOException statement is discussed in Chapter 5.

```
public static void main (String arg [ ]) throws IOException
{ // Define the input integer variable
  int intest = 0;
```

4. Use the Java Reader to read a number from the keyboard and store it in a variable called **input**. The number read is a string.

```
System.out.println ("If Else Select");
System.out.println (" ");
System.out.println ("Type a number between 0 and 100 and press
                    enter");
// Read an integer from the keyboard
String input = stdin.readLine ( );
```

5. Convert the numbers read from the keyboard to an integer and store it in a variable called **intest**.

```
intest = Integer.parseInt (input);
```

6. Write if-elsestatements to select the range of the number read from the keyboard. Count the number of times the range was selected. Sum the number selected in a range.

```
// Test for the range 0 to 25.
if ((intest >= 0) && (intest <= 25))
  { // Increment the range counter.
    cnt0_25 = cnt0_25 + 1;
    // Add the new within range value to the range sum.
    sum0_25 = sum0_25 + intest;
    // Read another integer from the keyboard.
  }

// Test for the range 26 to 60.
else
if ((intest > 25) && (intest <= 60))
  { // Increment the range counter.
    cnt26_60 = cnt26_60 + 1;
    // Add the new within range value to the range sum.
    sum26_60 = sum26_60 + intest;
    // Read another integer from the keyboard.
  }

// Test for the range 61 to 100.
else
if ((intest > 60) && (intest <= 100))
  { // Increment the range counter.
    cnt61_100 = cnt61_100 + 1;
    // Add the new within range value to the range sum.
    sum61_100 = sum61_100 + intest;
    // Read another integer from the keyboard.
  }
```

7. When a negative number is read from the keyboard write the results of the selected range and sum of the numbers in the selected range on the console. Terminate the program when a negative number is read.

```
if ((intest >= 0) && (intest <= 100))
  {System.out.println ("The count for range 0 to 25 is: " +
                       cnt0_25);
   System.out.println ("The sum for range 0 to 25 is: " +
                       sum0_25);
   System.out.println ("The count for range 26 to 60 is: " +
                       cnt26_60);
   System.out.println ("The sum for range 26 to 60 is: " +
                       sum26_60);
   System.out.println ("The count for range 61 to 100 is: " +
                       cnt61_100);
```

```
            System.out.println ("The sum for range 61 to 100 is: " +
                                sum61_100);
            System.exit (0);
         }
```

8. Define the tail of the Java main method.

   ```
   } // End main Method
   ```

9. Define the tail of the Java class elserang.

   ```
   } // End class elserang
   ```

Implemented application using if else statements that is saved in a file called **elserang.java**.

```
// elserang
// An application that uses if-else statements to select ranges
import java.io.*;
public class elserang
{
  // Define and initialize the count range variables
  private static int cnt0_25 = 0;
  private static int cnt26_60 = 0;
  private static int cnt61_100 = 0;
  // Define and initialize the sum range variables
  private static int sum0_25 = 0;
  private static int sum26_60 = 0;
  private static int sum61_100 = 0;

  // ----------------------
  // Other Java methods
  // ----------------------

  // Unique main Java method

  // Create a single shared BufferedReader for keyboard input
  private static BufferedReader stdin = new BufferedReader (new
  InputStreamReader (System.in));

  // The main Java Method
  public static void main (String arg [ ]) throws IOException
  { // Define the input integer variable
    int intest = 0;
```

```java
System.out.println("If Else Select");
System.out.println(" ");
System.out.println ("Type a number between 0 and 100 and press
                enter");
// Read an integer from the keyboard
String input = stdin.readLine ( );
// Convert input to an integer
intest = Integer.parseInt (input);

// Test for the range 0 to 25.
if ((intest >= 0) && (intest <= 25))
  { // Increment the range counter.
    cnt0_25 = cnt0_25 + 1;
    // Add the new within range value to the range sum.
    sum0_25 = sum0_25 + intest;
    // Read another integer from the keyboard.
  }

// Test for the range 26 to 60.
else
if ((intest > 25) && (intest <= 60))
  { // Increment the range counter.
    cnt26_60 = cnt26_60 + 1;
    // Add the new within range value to the range sum.
    sum26_60 = sum26_60 + intest;
    // Read another integer from the keyboard.
  }

// Test for the range 61 to 100.
else
if ((intest > 60) && (intest <= 100))
  { // Increment the range counter.
    cnt61_100 = cnt61_100 + 1;
    // Add the new within range value to the range sum.
    sum61_100 = sum61_100 + intest;
    // Read another integer from the keyboard.
  }

// Test for program termination. Write program results.

if ((intest >= 0) && (intest <= 100))
  { System.out.println ("The count for range 0 to 25 is: " +
                cnt0_25);
```

```
            System.out.println ("The sum for range 0 to 25 is: " +
                                sum0_25);
            System.out.println ("The count for range 26 to 60 is: " +
                                cnt26_60);
            System.out.println ("The sum for range 26 to 60 is: " +
                                sum26_60);
            System.out.println ("The count for range 61 to 100 is: " +
                                cnt61_100);
            System.out.println ("The sum for range 61 to 100 is: " +
                                sum61_100);
            System.exit (0);
        }
    } // End main Method
} // End class elserang
```

3.1.3. Shortcut if Statements

The shortcut form of the if statement syntax is

```
Variable = Boolean Expression ? true.result.expression :
           false.result.expression;
```

For example, the following statement assigns 6 to z if t is greater than 0 and -6 to z if t is less than or equal to 0.

```
if (t > 0) z = 6
else z = -6;
```

The result in shortcut form is

```
z = (t > 0) ? 6 : -6;
```

3.2. Using switch Statements

The Switch statement is a selection control structure that lists any number of branches. This structure allows multi-way branches. The value of the switch expression determines the switch label to select. Each branch is labeled to determine which one of the branches is executed. For example, examine the following statement:

```
switch (day)
{ case 'M' : Statement1; or {Statements}
                    break;
  case 'T' : Statement2; or {Statements}
                    break;
  case 'W' : Statement3; or {Statements}
                    break;
  case 'H' : Statement4; or {Statements}
                    break;
  case 'F' : Statement5; or {Statements}
                    break;
  case 'S' : Statement6; or {Statements}
                    break;
  case 'U' : Statement7; or {Statements}
                    break;

  default : Statement8; or {Statements}
}
Statement9;
```

In this example, day is the switch expression. If day is 'M', execute Statement1 or {Statements} and break out of the switch statement, continuing with Statement 9. The break statement causes an immediate exit from the Switch statement. If the switch expression evaluated to a label that is not in the Switch statement it executes the default label.

For example, write an application to read from the counsel six integers between 0 and 100. Use three integer variables to count the number of times the numbers read were in the ranges 0 to 25, 26 to 60, and 61 to 100. Sum the numbers read in each range. Exit the application when a negative integer is read.

Implementation of a select range steps using case statements are:

1. Implement a Java program that uses if-statements to select ranges call **caserang**. Define the class head with an import package and variable declarations. Java packages are discussed in Chapter 7.

```
import java.io.*;
public class caserang
{
   // Define and initialize the count range variables
   private static int cnt0_25 = 0;
```

```
private static int cnt26_60 = 0;
private static int cnt61_100 = 0;
// Define and initialize the sum range variables
private static int sum0_25 = 0;
private static int sum26_60 = 0;
private static int sum61_100 = 0;
```

2. Define a Java Reader to input data from the keyboard. BufferedReader is discussed in Chapter 6. Create a single shared BufferedReader for keyboard input.

    ```
    private static BufferedReader stdin = new BufferedReader(new InputStreamReader (System.in));
    ```

3. Define the head of the Java main method with variable declarations. The Java throws IOException statement is discussed in Chapter 5.

    ```
    // The main Java Method
    public static void main (String arg [ ]) throws IOException
    { // Define the input integer variable and a control variable.
      int intest = 0;
      int cval = 0;
    ```

4. Use the Java Reader to read a number from the keyboard and store it in a variable called **input**. The number read is a string.

    ```
    System.out.println ("Case Select");
    System.out.println (" ");
    System.out.println ("Type a number between 0 and 100 and press
                        enter");
    // Read a line of text from the user.
    String input = stdin.readLine ( );
    ```

5. Convert the numbers read from the keyboard to an integer and store it in a variable called **intest**.

    ```
    intest = Integer.parseInt (input);
    ```

6. Write if-statements to select the range of the number read from the keyboard. Count the number of times the range was selected. Sum the number selected in a range.

```
cval = 0;
if (intest < 0) cval = 1;
if ((intest >= 0) && (intest <= 25)) cval = 2;
if ((intest > 25) && (intest <= 60)) cval = 3;
if ((intest > 60) && (intest <= 100)) cval = 4;

switch (cval)
{ // Test for the range 0 to 25.
  case 2:
    // Increment the range counter.
    cnt0_25 = cnt0_25 + 1;
    // Add the new within range value to the range sum.
    sum0_25 = sum0_25 + intest;
    // Read another integer from the keyboard.
    break;

  // Test for the range 26 to 60.
  case 3:
    // Increment the range counter.
    cnt26_60 = cnt26_60 + 1;
    // Add the new within range value to the range sum.
    sum26_60 = sum26_60 + intest;
    // Read another integer from the keyboard.
    break;

  // Test for the range 61 to 100.
  case 4:
    // Increment the range counter.
    cnt61_100 = cnt61_100 + 1;
    // Add the new within range value to the range sum.
    sum61_100 = sum61_100 + intest;
    // Read another integer from the keyboard.
    break;
} // End case Statement
```

7. When a negative number is read from the keyboard write the results with out count and sum of the selected range is written on the console. Positive numbers in the selected range are counted and summed before they are written on the console.

```
    // Test for program termination. Write program results.
    System.out.println ("The count for range 0 to 25 is: " +
                        cnt0_25);
    System.out.println ("The sum for range 0 to 25 is: " +
                        sum0_25);
    System.out.println ("The count for range 26 to 60 is: " +
                        cnt26_60);
    System.out.println ("The sum for range 26 to 60 is: " +
                        sum26_60);
    System.out.println ("The count for range 61 to 100 is: " +
                        cnt61_100);
    System.out.println ("The sum for range 61 to 100 is: " +
                        sum61_100);
    System.exit (0);
```

8. Define the tail of the Java main method.

   ```
   } // End main Method
   ```

9. Define the tail of the Java class caserang.

   ```
   } // End class caserang
   ```

Implemented application using case statements that is saved in a file called **caserang.java**.

```
// caserang
// An application that uses case statements to select ranges
import java.io.*;
public class caserang
{
  // Define and initialize the count range variables
  private static int cnt0_25 = 0;
  private static int cnt26_60 = 0;
  private static int cnt61_100 = 0;
  // Define and initialize the sum range variables
  private static int sum0_25 = 0;
  private static int sum26_60 = 0;
  private static int sum61_100 = 0;

  // Create a single shared BufferedReader for keyboard input
  private static BufferedReader stdin = new BufferedReader (new
  InputStreamReader (System.in));
```

```java
// The main Java Method
public static void main (String arg [ ]) throws IOException
{ // Define the input integer variable and a control variable.
  int intest = 0;
  int cval = 0;
  // Read an integer from the keyboard
  System.out.println ("Case Select");
  System.out.println (" ");
  // Prompt the user
  System.out.println ("Type a number between 0 and 100 and press
                  enter");
  // Read a line of text from the user.
  String input = stdin.readLine ( );
  // Convert the etring to integer
  intest = Integer.parseInt (input);
  cval = 0;
  if (intest < 0) cval = 1;
  if ((intest >= 0) && (intest <= 25)) cval = 2;
  if ((intest > 25) && (intest <= 60)) cval = 3;
  if ((intest > 60) && (intest <= 100)) cval = 4;

  switch (cval)
  { // Test for the range 0 to 25.
    case 2:
      // Increment the range counter.
      cnt0_25 = cnt0_25 + 1;
      // Add the new within range value to the range sum.
      sum0_25 = sum0_25 + intest;
      // Read another integer from the keyboard.
      break;

    // Test for the range 26 to 60.
    case 3:
      // Increment the range counter.
      cnt26_60 = cnt26_60 + 1;
      // Add the new within range value to the range sum.
      sum26_60 = sum26_60 + intest;
      // Read another integer from the keyboard.
      break;

    // Test for the range 61 to 100.
    case 4:
      // Increment the range counter.
      cnt61_100 = cnt61_100 + 1;
```

```
            // Add the new within range value to the range sum.
            sum61_100 = sum61_100 + intest;
            // Read another integer from the keyboard.
            break;
        } // End case Statement

        // Test for program termination. Write program results.
        System.out.println ("The count for range 0 to 25 is: " +
                            cnt0_25);
        System.out.println ("The sum for range 0 to 25 is: " +
                            sum0_25);
        System.out.println ("The count for range 26 to 60 is: " +
                            cnt26_60);
        System.out.println ("The sum for range 26 to 60 is: " +
                            sum26_60);
        System.out.println ("The count for range 61 to 100 is: " +
                            cnt61_100);
        System.out.println ("The sum for range 61 to 100 is: " +
                            sum61_100);
        System.exit (0);

    } // End main Method
} // End class caserang
```

3.3. Using Loop Structures

Loops are structures that control repeated execution of a segment of code. The part of the loop that is executed repeatedly is called the **loop body**. The loop body may be a single statement; or {statements}. Each time the loop body is executed it is called an iteration of the loop. Each loop contains a continue-condition that is a Boolean expression that is evaluated in the iteration. If the condition is true, the body is executed as another iterate. If the condition is false, the loop terminates the iteration process. The Java programming language supports a for loop, while loop, and a do loop;

3.3.1. The for Loop

For loop is a production that causes the loop body to be repeated for a fixed number of times. A for loop syntax is detailed in Figure 14.

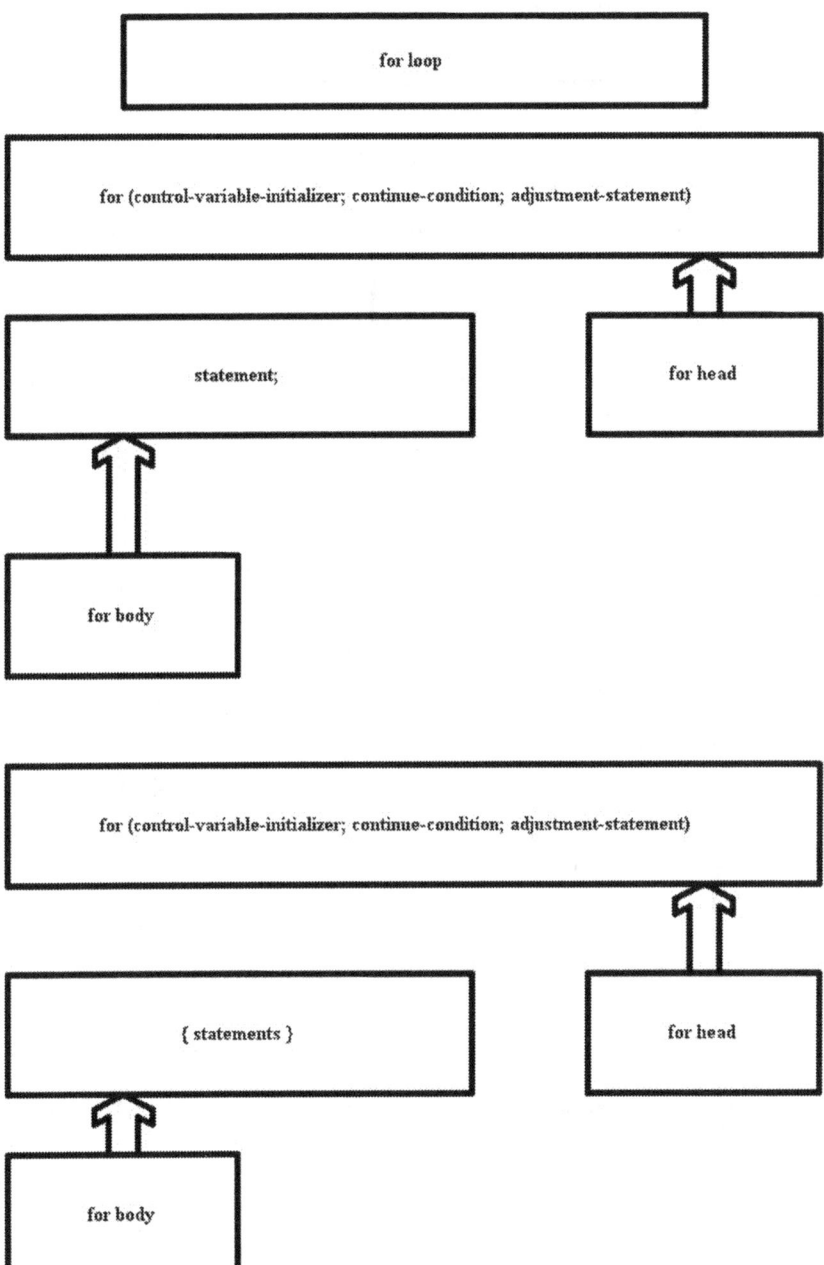

Figure 14. for Loop Syntax

A for loop flow of control is detailed in Figure 15.

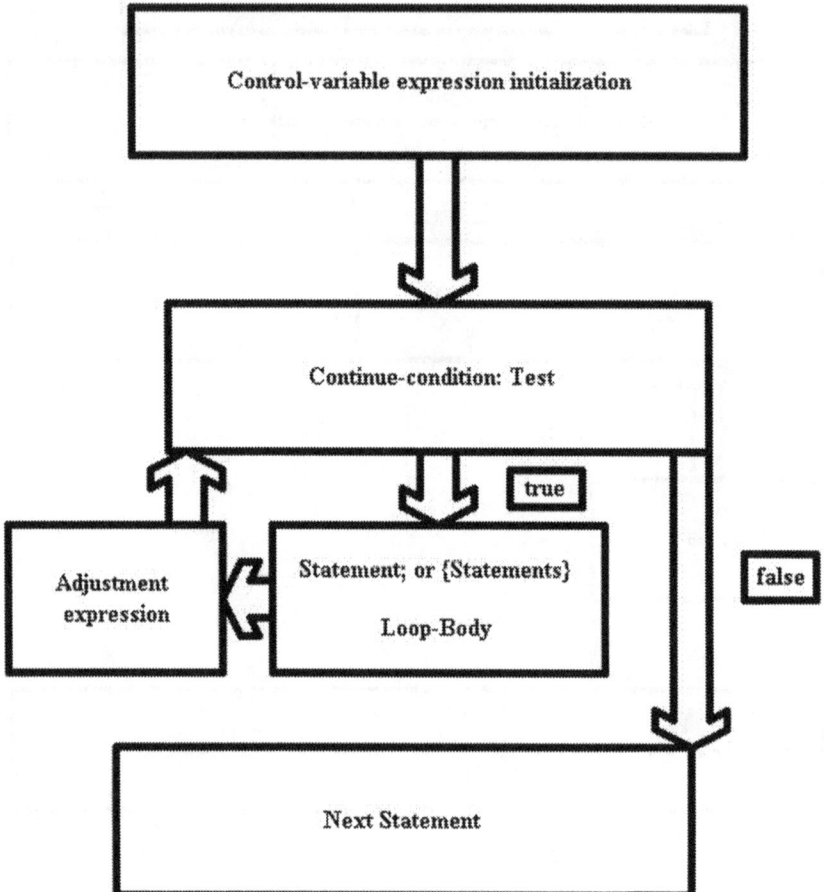

Figure 15. for Loop Flow of Control

For example, the following code segment uses a **for loop** to print Hello Java 50 times.

```
int j;
for (j = 0; j < 50; j++)
{ System.out.println ("Hello Java");
}
```

For example, write an application to read from the counsel six integers between 0 and 100. Use three integer variables to count the number of times the numbers read were in the ranges 0 to 25, 26 to 60, and 61 to 100. Sum the numbers read in each range. Exit the application when a negative integer is read.

Implement the application using for statement. An upper bound on the number of integers that will be read is necessary to implement the application with for statements. Assume that the maximum number of integers read is 1000.

Implementation of a select range steps using for loop and if statements are:

1. Implement a Java program that uses for loop and if statements to select ranges call **forrang**. Define the class head with an import package and variable declarations. Java packages are discussed in Chapter 7.

   ```
   import java.io.*;
   public class forrang
   {
      // Define and initialize the count range variables
      private static int cnt0_25 = 0;
      private static int cnt26_60 = 0;
      private static int cnt61_100 = 0;
      // Define and initialize the sum range variables
      private static int sum0_25 = 0;
      private static int sum26_60 = 0;
      private static int sum61_100 = 0;
   ```

2. Define a Java Reader to input data from the keyboard. Create a single shared BufferedReader for keyboard input. BufferedReader is discussed in Chapter 6.

   ```
   private static BufferedReader stdin = new BufferedReader (new InputStreamReader (System.in));
   ```

3. Define the head of the Java main method with variable declarations. The Java throws IOException statement is discussed in Chapter 5.

   ```
   public static void main (String arg [ ]) throws IOException
   { // Define the input integer variable
      int intest = 30;
   ```

4. Use the Java Reader to read a number from the keyboard and store it in a variable called **input**. The number read is a string. Read the numbers in a bounded for loop.

```
System.out.println ("For Loop");
System.out.println (" ");
// Define the for loop head
for (int I = 0; I < 1000; ++I)
{
   // Read an integer from the keyboard
   System.out.println ("Type a number between 0 and 100 and
                       press enter");
   System.out.println ("Type a negative number to terminate the
                       program and press enter");
   // Read a line of text from the user.
   String input = stdin.readLine ( );
```

5. Convert the numbers read from the keyboard to an integer and store it in a variable called **intest**.

```
intest = Integer.parseInt (input);
```

6. Write if statements to select the range of the number read from the keyboard. Count the number of times the range was selected. Sum the number selected in a Range variable Terminate the program when a negative number is read and write a report for the range counts and sums.

```
if (intest < 0)
  { System.out.println ("The count for range 0 to 25 is: " +
                        cnt0_25);
    System.out.println ("The sum for range 0 to 25 is: " +
                        sum0_25);
    System.out.println ("The count for range 26 to 60 is: "
                        + cnt26_60);
    System.out.println ("The sum for range 26 to 60 is: " +
                        sum26_60);
    System.out.println ("The count for range 61 to 100 is: "
                        + cnt61_100);
    System.out.println ("The sum for range 61 to 100 is: " +
                        sum61_100);
    System.exit (0);
  }
```

```
// Test for the range 0 to 25.
if ((intest >= 0) && (intest <= 25))
  { // Increment the range counter.
    cnt0_25 = cnt0_25 + 1;
    // Add the new within range value to the range sum.
    sum0_25 = sum0_25 + intest;
    // Read another integer from the keyboard.
  }

// Test for the range 26 to 60.
if ((intest > 25) && (intest <= 60))
  { // Increment the range counter.
    cnt26_60 = cnt26_60 + 1;
    // Add the new within range value to the range sum.
    sum26_60 = sum26_60 + intest;
    // Read another integer from the keyboard.
    intest = -1;
  }

// Test for the range 61 to 100.
if ((intest > 60) && (intest <= 100))
  { // Increment the range counter.
    cnt61_100 = cnt61_100 + 1;
    // Add the new within range value to the range sum.
    sum61_100 = sum61_100 + intest;
    // Read another integer from the keyboard.
  }
```

7. Define for loop tail.

   ```
   } // End for loop
   ```

8. Define the tail of the Java main method.

   ```
   } // End main Method
   ```

9. Define the tail of the Java class forrang.

   ```
   } // End class forrang
   ```

Implemented application using if else statements and save it in a file called **forrang.java.**

```java
// forrang
// An application that uses for statements to select ranges
import java.io.*;
public class forrang
{
  // Define and initialize the count range variables
  private static int cnt0_25 = 0;
  private static int cnt26_60 = 0;
  private static int cnt61_100 = 0;
  // Define and initialize the sum range variables
  private static int sum0_25 = 0;
  private static int sum26_60 = 0;
  private static int sum61_100 = 0;

  // Create a single shared BufferedReader for keyboard input
  private static BufferedReader stdin = new BufferedReader (new
  InputStreamReader (System.in));

  // The main Java Method
  public static void main (String arg [ ]) throws IOException
  { // Define the input integer variable
    int intest = 30;
    System.out.println ("For Loop");
    System.out.println (" ");
    // Define the for loop head
    for (int i = 0; i < 1000; ++i)
    {
      // Read an integer from the keyboard
      // Prompt the user
      System.out.println ("Type a number between 0 and 100 and
                          press enter");
      System.out.println ("Type a negative number to termoinate
                          the program and press enter");
      // Read a line of text from the user.
      String input = stdin.readLine ( );
      // Convert the string to an integer
      intest = Integer.parseInt (input);

      // Test for program termination. Write program results.
      if (intest < 0)
        { System.out.println ("The count for range 0 to 25 is: " +
                          cnt0_25);
```

```java
            System.out.println ("The sum for range 0 to 25 is: " +
                                sum0_25);
            System.out.println ("The count for range 26 to 60 is: "
                                + cnt26_60);
            System.out.println ("The sum for range 26 to 60 is: " +
                                sum26_60);
            System.out.println ("The count for range 61 to 100 is: "
                                + cnt61_100);
            System.out.println ("The sum for range 61 to 100 is: " +
                                sum61_100);
            System.exit (0);
          }

        // Test for the range 0 to 25.
        if ((intest >= 0) && (intest <= 25))
          { // Increment the range counter.
            cnt0_25 = cnt0_25 + 1;
            // Add the new within range value to the range sum.
            sum0_25 = sum0_25 + intest;
            // Read another integer from the keyboard.
          }
        // Test for the range 26 to 60.
        if ((intest > 25) && (intest <= 60))
          { // Increment the range counter.
            cnt26_60 = cnt26_60 + 1;
            // Add the new within range value to the range sum.
            sum26_60 = sum26_60 + intest;
            // Read another integer from the keyboard.
            intest = -1;
          }
        // Test for the range 61 to 100.
        if ((intest > 60) && (intest <= 100))
          { // Increment the range counter.
            cnt61_100 = cnt61_100 + 1;
            // Add the new within range value to the range sum.
            sum61_100 = sum61_100 + intest;
            // Read another integer from the keyboard.
          }
      } // End for loop
    } // End main Method
} // End class forrang
```

A screen view of the forrang class execution with inputs 20, 40, 30, 60, 85, and -3 is:

```
C:\j2sdk1.4.2_04\bin\java.exe - Finished
For Loop
Type a number between 0 and 100 and press enter
Type a negative number to terminate the program and press enter
20
Type a number between 0 and 100 and press enter
Type a negative number to terminate the program and press enter
40
Type a number between 0 and 100 and press enter
Type a negative number to terminate the program and press enter
30
Type a number between 0 and 100 and press enter
Type a negative number to terminate the program and press enter
60
Type a number between 0 and 100 and press enter
Type a negative number to terminate the program and press enter
85
Type a number between 0 and 100 and press enter
Type a negative number to terminate the program and press enter
-3
The count for range 0 to 25 is:   1
The sum for range 0 to 25 is:   20
The count for range 26 to 60 is:   3
The sum for range 26 to 60 is:   130
The count for range 61 to 100 is:   1
The sum for range 61 to 100 is:   85
```

3.3.2. The while Loop

For loop was examined in detail in the Section 3.3.1. In for loop the control-variable expression is adjusted with an expression in the syntax of the head of the loop. While loop differs from for loop in that the control-variable expression is adjusted in the body of the while loop. Initialization of the control-variable is in the head of for loop and before entering the head of while loops. The test condition of for loop and the while loop is in the head of the loops. A while loop syntax is detailed in Figure 16.

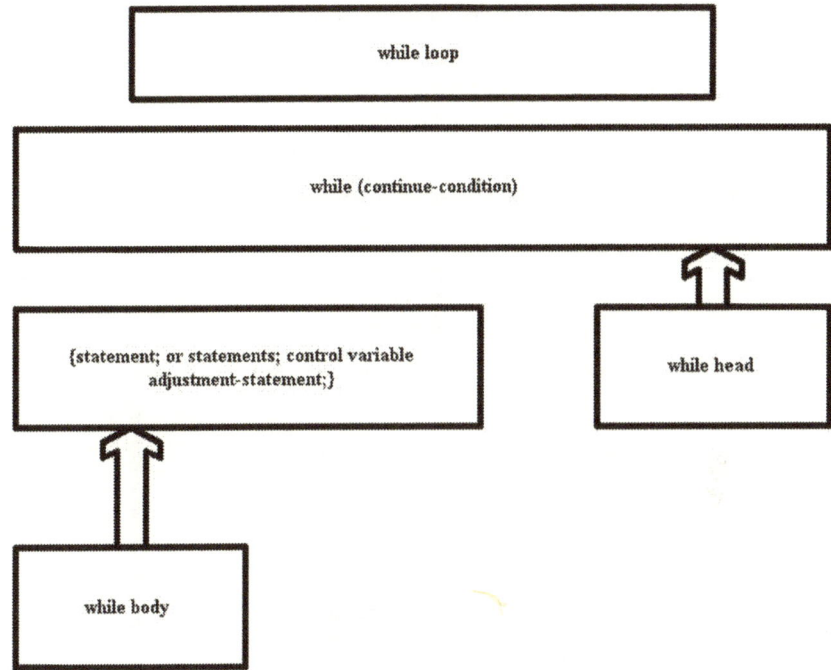

Figure 16. while Loop Syntax

A while loop flow of control is detailed in Figure 17.

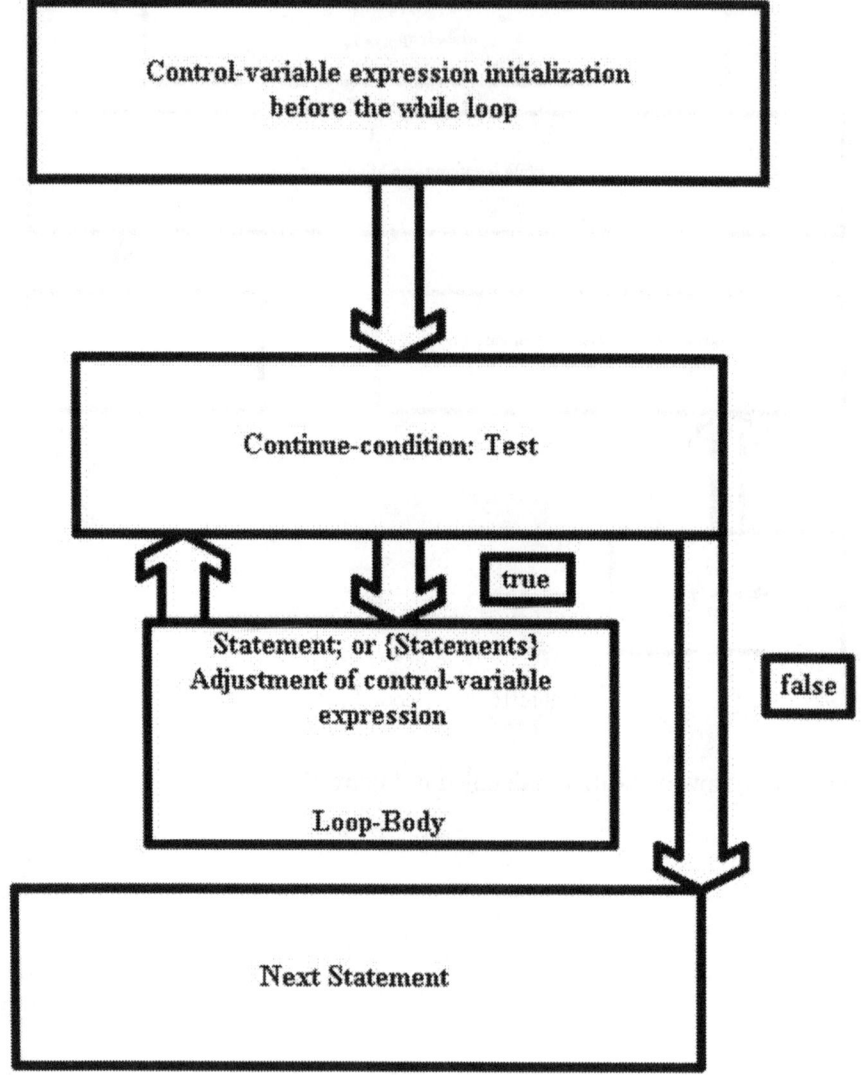

Figure 17. while loop Flow of Control

For example, the following code segment uses a while loop to print Hello Java 50 times.

```java
int j;
j = 0;
while (j < 50)
{ System.out.println ("Hello Java");
  // Increment the control-variable expression
  j = j + 1;
}
```

For example, write an application to read from the counsel six integers between 0 and 100. Use three integer variables to count the number of times the numbers read were in the ranges 0 to 25, 26 to 60, and 61 to 100. Sum the numbers read in each range. Exit the application when a negative integer is read.

Implement the application using while statement. A sentinel variable is used to control the while loop. This differs from for loop that required a fixed known upper bound on the loop.

Implementation of a select range steps using while loop and if statements are:

1. Implement a Java program that uses for loop and if statements to select ranges call **wrange**. Define the class head with an import package and variable declarations. Java packages are discussed in Chapter 7.

   ```java
   import java.io.*;
   public class wrange
   {
      // Define and initialize the count range variables
      private static int cnt0_25 = 0;
      private static int cnt26_60 = 0;
      private static int cnt61_100 = 0;
      // Define and initialize the sum range variables
      private static int sum0_25 = 0;
      private static int sum26_60 = 0;
      private static int sum61_100 = 0;
   ```

2. Define a Java Reader to input data from the keyboard. Create a single shared BufferedReader for keyboard input. BufferedReader is discussed in Chapter 6.

```
// Create a single shared BufferedReader for keyboard input
private static BufferedReader stdin = new BufferedReader (new
InputStreamReader (System.in));
```

3. Define the head of the Java main method with variable declarations. The Java throws IOException statement is discussed in Chapter 5.

   ```
   public static void main (String arg [ ]) throws IOException
   { // Define the input integer variable
     int intest = 0;
     // Define a sentinel variable to control the while loop.
     int wcontrol = 10;
   ```

4. Use the Java Reader to read a number from the keyboard and store it in a variable called **input**. The number read is a string.

   ```
   System.out.println ("While Loop");
   System.out.println (" ");
   // Define the while loop head
   while (wcontrol >= 0)
   {
      // Read an integer from the keyboard
      System.out.println ("Type a number between 0 and 100 and
                          press enter");
      System.out.println ("Type a negative number to terminate the
                          program and press enter");
      // Read a line of text from the user.
      String input = stdin.readLine ( );
   ```

5. Convert the numbers read from the keyboard to an integer and store it in a variable called **intest**.

   ```
   // Convert the string to an integer
   intest = Integer.parseInt (input);
   ```

6. Write if statements to select the range of the number read from the keyboard. Count the number of times the range was selected. Sum the number selected in a Range variable Terminate the program when a negative number is read and write a report for the range counts and sums.

   ```
   // Test for program termination. Write program results.
   if (intest < 0)
     { System.out.println ("The count for range 0 to 25 is: " +
                           cnt0_25);
   ```

```
            System.out.println ("The sum for range 0 to 25 is: " +
                                sum0_25);
            System.out.println ("The count for range 26 to 60 is: "
                                + cnt26_60);
            System.out.println ("The sum for range 26 to 60 is: " +
                                sum26_60);
            System.out.println ("The count for range 61 to 100 is: "
                                + cnt61_100);
            System.out.println ("The sum for range 61 to 100 is: " +
                                sum61_100);
            wcontrol = -1;
            break;
          }

        // Test for the range 0 to 25.
        if (intest <= 25)
          { // Increment the range counter.
            cnt0_25 = cnt0_25 + 1;
            // Add the new within range value to the range sum.
            sum0_25 = sum0_25 + intest;
            // Read another integer from the keyboard.
          }
        // Test for the range 26 to 60.
        if ((intest > 25) && (intest <= 60))
          { // Increment the range counter.
            cnt26_60 = cnt26_60 + 1;
            // Add the new within range value to the range sum.
            sum26_60 = sum26_60 + intest;
            // Read another integer from the keyboard.
          }
        // Test for the range 61 to 100.
        if ((intest > 60) && (intest <= 100))
          { // Increment the range counter.
            cnt61_100 = cnt61_100 + 1;
            // Add the new within range value to the range sum.
            sum61_100 = sum61_100 + intest;
            // Read another integer from the keyboard.
          }
```

7. Define while loop tail.

```
        } // End while loop
        System.exit (0);
```

8. Define the tail of the Java main method.

   ```
   } // End main Method
   ```

9. Define the tail of the Java class wrange.

   ```
   } // End class wrange
   ```

Implemented application using while loop that is saved in a file called **wrange.java**.

```
// wrange
// An application that uses a while loop statements to select ranges
import java.io.*;
public class wrange
{
  // Define and initialize the count range variables
  private static int cnt0_25 = 0;
  private static int cnt26_60 = 0;
  private static int cnt61_100 = 0;
  // Define and initialize the sum range variables
  private static int sum0_25 = 0;
  private static int sum26_60 = 0;
  private static int sum61_100 = 0;

  // Create a single shared BufferedReader for keyboard input
  private static BufferedReader stdin = new BufferedReader (new
  InputStreamReader (System.in));

  // The main Java Method
  public static void main (String arg [ ]) throws IOException
  { // Define the input integer variable
    int intest = 0;
    // Define a sentinel variable to control the while loop.
    int wcontrol = 10;
    System.out.println ("While Loop");
    System.out.println (" ");
    // Define the while loop head
    while (wcontrol >= 0)
    {
      // Read an integer from the keyboard
      System.out.println ("Type a number between 0 and 100 and
                          press enter");
      System.out.println ("Type a negative number to terminate the
                          program and press enter");
```

```java
    // Read a line of text from the user.
    String input = stdin.readLine ( );
    // Convert the string to an integer
    intest = Integer.parseInt (input);

    // Test for program termination. Write program results.
    if (intest < 0)
      { System.out.println ("The count for range 0 to 25 is: " +
                            cnt0_25);
        System.out.println ("The sum for range 0 to 25 is: " +
                            sum0_25);
        System.out.println ("The count for range 26 to 60 is: "
                            + cnt26_60);
        System.out.println ("The sum for range 26 to 60 is: " +
                            sum26_60);
        System.out.println ("The count for range 61 to 100 is: "
                            + cnt61_100);
        System.out.println ("The sum for range 61 to 100 is: " +
                            sum61_100);
        wcontrol = -1;
        break;
      }

    // Test for the range 0 to 25.
    if (intest <= 25)
      { // Increment the range counter.
        cnt0_25 = cnt0_25 + 1;
        // Add the new within range value to the range sum.
        sum0_25 = sum0_25 + intest;
        // Read another integer from the keyboard.
      }
    // Test for the range 26 to 60.
    if ((intest > 25) && (intest <= 60))
      { // Increment the range counter.
        cnt26_60 = cnt26_60 + 1;
        // Add the new within range value to the range sum.
        sum26_60 = sum26_60 + intest;
        // Read another integer from the keyboard.
      }
    // Test for the range 61 to 100.
    if ((intest > 60) && (intest <= 100))
      { // Increment the range counter.
        cnt61_100 = cnt61_100 + 1;
        // Add the new within range value to the range sum.
        sum61_100 = sum61_100 + intest;
```

```
            // Read another integer from the keyboard.
        }
    } // End while loop
    System.exit (0);
  } // End main Method
} // End class wrange
```

A screen view of the wrange class execution with inputs 45, 22, 38, 64, 97, and -2 is:

```
C:\j2sdk1.4.2_04\bin\java.exe - Finished
While Loop
Type a number between 0 and 100 and press enter
Type a negative number to terminate the program and press enter
45
Type a number between 0 and 100 and press enter
Type a negative number to terminate the program and press enter
22
Type a number between 0 and 100 and press enter
Type a negative number to terminate the program and press enter
38
Type a number between 0 and 100 and press enter
Type a negative number to terminate the program and press enter
64
Type a number between 0 and 100 and press enter
Type a negative number to terminate the program and press enter
97
Type a number between 0 and 100 and press enter
Type a negative number to terminate the program and press enter
-2
The count for range 0 to 25 is:  1
The sum for range 0 to 25 is:    22
The count for range 26 to 60 is:  2
The sum for range 26 to 60 is:   83
The count for range 61 to 100 is:  2
The sum for range 61 to 100 is:  161
```

3.3.3. The do Loop

The do loop syntax is similar to the while loop. The basic difference is that the test condition is after the do loop body. Test condition is performed before the loop body in while loop. Adjustments to the control-variable expression are made in the loop body of while loop and do loop. Initialization of the control-variable expression occurs before the loop body. A do loop syntax is detailed in Figure 18.

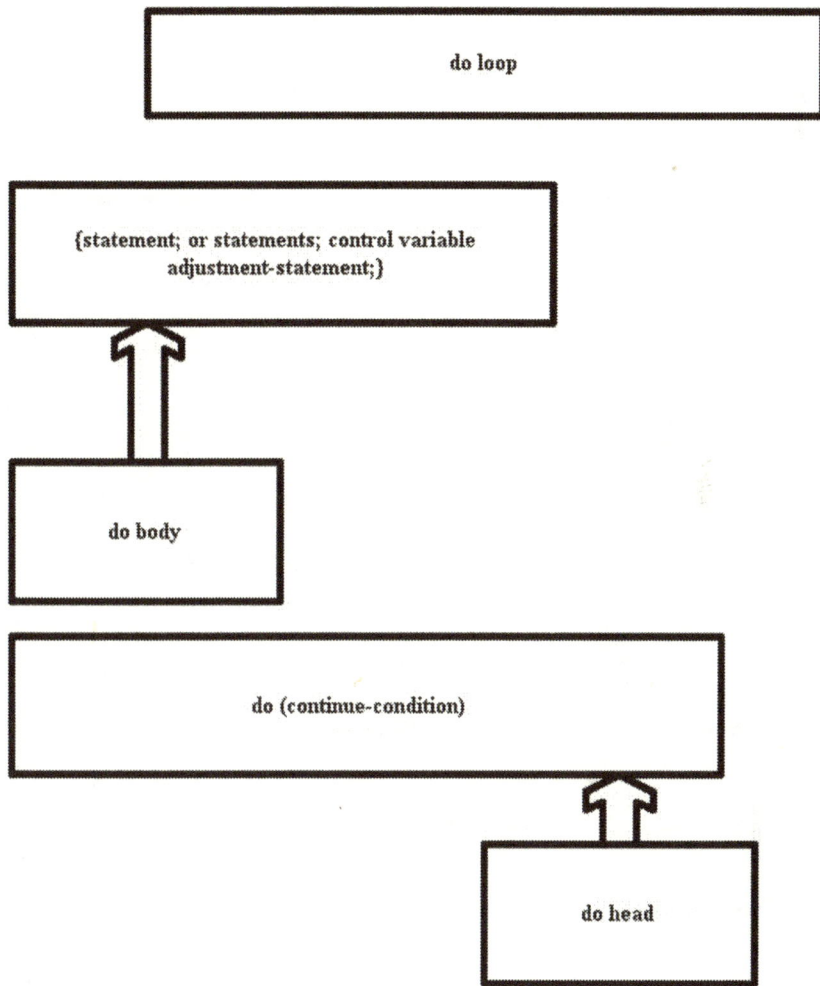

Figure 18. do loop Syntax

A do loop flow of control is detailed in Figure 19.

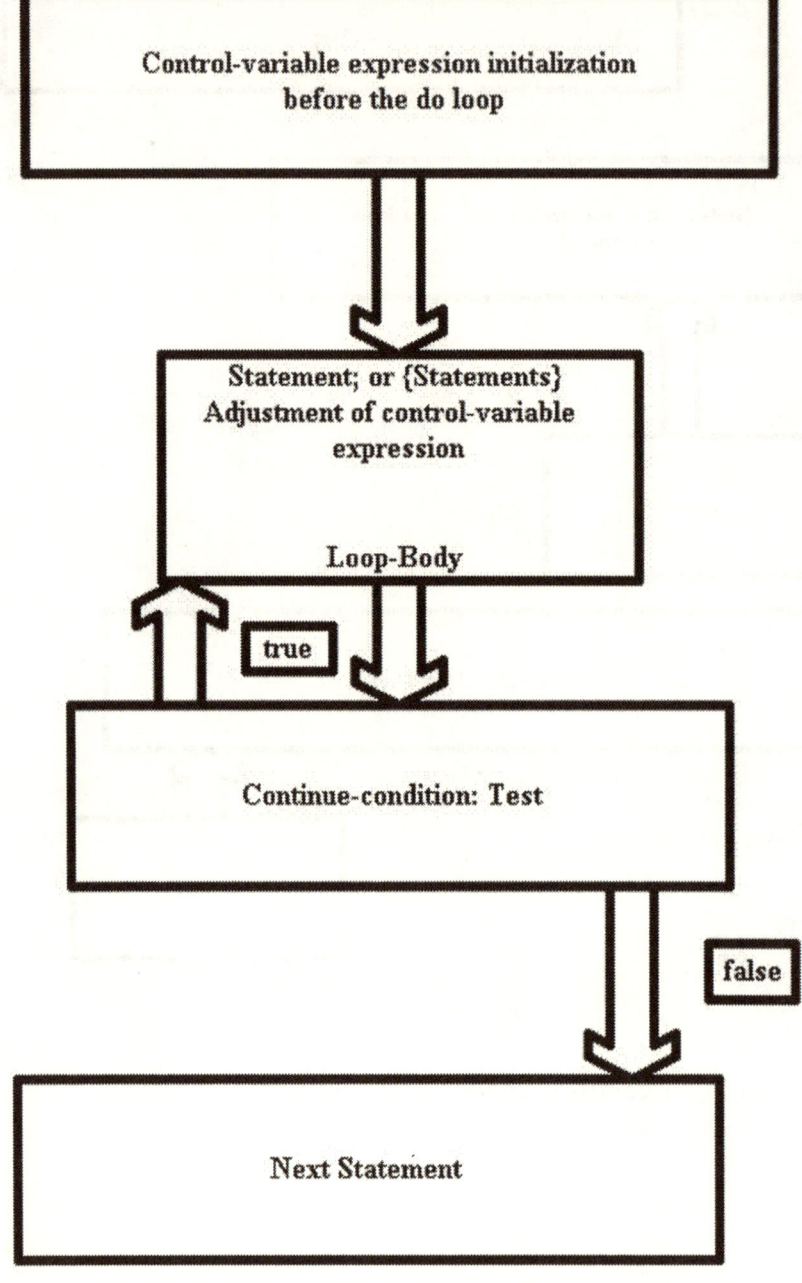

Figure 19. do loop Flow of Control

For example, the following code segment uses a do loop to print Hello Java 50 times.

```
int j;
j = 0;
do
{ System.out.println ("Hello Java");
  // Increment the control-variable expression
  j = j + 1;
} while (j < 50);
```

For example, write an application to read from the counsel six integers between 0 and 100. Use three integer variables to count the number of times the numbers read were in the ranges 0 to 25, 26 to 60, and 61 to 100. Sum the numbers read in each range. Exit the application when a negative integer is read.

Implement the application using do statement. A sentinel variable is used to control the do loop. This differs from for loop that required a fixed known upper bound on the loop.

Implementation of a select range steps using do loop and if statements are:

1. Implement a Java program that uses for loop and if statements to select ranges call **dorange**. Define the class head with an import package and variable declarations. Java packages are discussed in Chapter 7.

   ```
   import java.io.*;
   public class dorange
   {
       // Define and initialize the count range variables
       private static int cnt0_25 = 0;
       private static int cnt26_60 = 0;
       private static int cnt61_100 = 0;
       // Define and initialize the sum range variables
       private static int sum0_25 = 0;
       private static int sum26_60 = 0;
       private static int sum61_100 = 0;
   ```

2. Define a Java Reader to input data from the keyboard. Create a single shared BufferedReader for keyboard input. BufferedReader is discussed in Chapter 6.

```
    private static BufferedReader stdin = new BufferedReader (new
    InputStreamReader (System.in));
```

3. Define the head of the Java main method with variable declarations. The Java throws IOException statement is discussed in Chapter 5.

```
    public static void main (String arg [ ]) throws IOException
    { // Define the input integer variable
      int intest = 0;
      // Define a sentinel variable to control the while loop.
      int wcontrol = 10;
```

4. Use the Java Reader to read a number from the keyboard and store it in a variable called **input**. The number read is a string. Define the do loop for reading data.

```
    System.out.println ("Do Loop");
    System.out.println (" ");
    do
    {
      // Read an integer from the keyboard
      System.out.println ("Type a number between 0 an 100 and
                          press enter");
      System.out.println ("Type a negative number to terminate the
                          program and press enter");
      // Read a line of text from the user.
      String input = stdin.readLine ( );
```

5. Convert the number read from the keyboard to an integer and store it in a variable called **intest**.

```
        intest = Integer.parseInt (input);
```

6. Write if statements to select the range of the number read from the keyboard. Count the number of times the range was selected. Sum the number selected in a Range variable Terminate the program when a negative number is read and write a report for the range counts and sums.

```
            // Test for program termination. Write program results.
            if (intest < 0)
              { System.out.println ("The count for range 0 to 25 is: " +
                                  cnt0_25);
                System.out.println ("The sum for range 0 to 25 is: " +
                                  sum0_25);
```

```
                System.out.println ("The count for range 26 to 60 is: "
                                  + cnt26_60);
                System.out.println ("The sum for range 26 to 60 is: " +
                                  sum26_60);
                System.out.println ("The count for range 61 to 100 is: "
                                  + cnt61_100);
                System.out.println ("The sum for range 61 to 100 is: " +
                                  sum61_100);
                wcontrol = -1;
                break;
            }

        // Test for the range 0 to 25.
        if ((intest >= 0) && (intest <= 25))
          { // Increment the range counter.
            cnt0_25 = cnt0_25 + 1;
            // Add the new within range value to the range sum.
            sum0_25 = sum0_25 + intest;
            // Read another integer from the keyboard.
          }
        // Test for the range 26 to 60.
        if ((intest > 25) && (intest <= 60))
          { // Increment the range counter.
            cnt26_60 = cnt26_60 + 1;
            // Add the new within range value to the range sum.
            sum26_60 = sum26_60 + intest;
            // Read another integer from the keyboard.
          }
        // Test for the range 61 to 100.
        if ((intest > 60) && (intest <= 100))
          { // Increment the range counter.
            cnt61_100 = cnt61_100 + 1;
            // Add the new within range value to the range sum.
            sum61_100 = sum61_100 + intest;
            // Read another integer from the keyboard.
          }
```

7. Define do while loop tail.

```
        } while (wcontrol >= 0);

        System.exit(0);
```

8. Define the tail of the Java main method.

   ```
   } // End main Method
   ```

9. Define the tail of the Java class dorange.

   ```
   } // End class dorange
   ```

Implemented application using do loop that is saved in a file called dorange.java.

```
// dorange
// An application that uses a while loop statements to select ranges
import java.io.*;
public class dorange
{
  // Define and initialize the count range variables
  private static int cnt0_25 = 0;
  private static int cnt26_60 = 0;
  private static int cnt61_100 = 0;
  // Define and initialize the sum range variables
  private static int sum0_25 = 0;
  private static int sum26_60 = 0;
  private static int sum61_100 = 0;

  // Create a single shared BufferedReader for keyboard input
  private static BufferedReader stdin = new BufferedReader(new InputStreamReader(System.in));

  // The main Java Method
  public static void main (String arg [ ]) throws IOException
  { // Define the input integer variable
    int intest = 0;
    // Define a sentinel variable to control the while loop.
    int wcontrol = 10;
    System.out.println ("Do Loop");
    System.out.println (" ");
    // Define the do loop
    do
    {
      // Read an integer from the keyboard
      System.out.println ("Type a number between 0 an 100 and
                          press enter");
```

```
System.out.println ("Type a negative number to terminate the
                    program and press enter");
// Read a line of text from the user.
String input = stdin.readLine ( );
// Convert the string to an integer
intest = Integer.parseInt (input);

// Test for program termination. Write program results.
if (intest < 0)
  { System.out.println ("The count for range 0 to 25 is: " +
                       cnt0_25);
    System.out.println ("The sum for range 0 to 25 is: " +
                       sum0_25);
    System.out.println ("The count for range 26 to 60 is: "
                       + cnt26_60);
    System.out.println ("The sum for range 26 to 60 is: " +
                       sum26_60);
    System.out.println ("The count for range 61 to 100 is: "
                       + cnt61_100);
    System.out.println ("The sum for range 61 to 100 is: " +
                       sum61_100);
    wcontrol = -1;
    break;
  }

// Test for the range 0 to 25.
if ((intest >= 0) && (intest <= 25))
  { // Increment the range counter.
    cnt0_25 = cnt0_25 + 1;
    // Add the new within range value to the range sum.
    sum0_25 = sum0_25 + intest;
    // Read another integer from the keyboard.
  }
// Test for the range 26 to 60.
  if ((intest > 25) && (intest <= 60))
  { // Increment the range counter.
    cnt26_60 = cnt26_60 + 1;
    // Add the new within range value to the range sum.
    sum26_60 = sum26_60 + intest;
    // Read another integer from the keyboard.
  }
// Test for the range 61 to 100.
if ((intest > 60) && (intest <= 100))
  { // Increment the range counter.
    cnt61_100 = cnt61_100 + 1;
```

```
            // Add the new within range value to the range sum.
            sum61_100 = sum61_100 + intest;
            // Read another integer from the keyboard.
        }
    } while (wcontrol >= 0);

    System.exit(0);
    } // End main Method
} // End class dorange
```

3.4. Using the Keywords break and continue

Additional controls used in loops are break and continue. The keyword break immediately ends the innermost loop that contains the break. Continue ends the current iteration. Program control goes to the next cycle of the loop.

For example, the following code segment uses a do loop with break to print Hello Java 49 times.

```
int j;
j = 0;
do
{ System.out.println ("Hello Java");
  // Increment the control-variable expression
  j = j + 1;
  if (j == 49) break;
} while (j < 50);
```

For example, the following code segment uses a do loop with continue to print Hello Java 49 times.

```
int j;
j = 0;
do
{ if (j >= 49) continue;
  System.out.println ("Hello Java");
  // Increment the control-variable expression
  j = j + 1;
} while (j < 50);
```

3.5. Exercises

1. Write a program that inputs a single letter and displays the corresponding digits on the telephone. The letters and digits on a telephone are 2-ABC, 3-DEF, 4-GHI, 5-JKL, 6-MNO, 7-PRS, 8-TUV, and 9-WXY. Display an error message for letters with no digit mappings.

2. Write a program to compute the date for any Easter Sunday from 1982 to 2048.

   > a is year % 19
   > b is year % 4
   > c is year % 7
   > d is (19 * a + 24) % 30
   > e is (2 * b + 4 * c + 6 * d + 5) % 7
   > Easter Sunday is March (22 + d + e)

   The program input is the year. The output is Easter Sunday for that year. Display an error message for out of range years.

3. Write a program that inputs an integer larger than 1 and calculates the sum of the squares from 1 to that integer. For example, if the integer is 6, the sum of the squares is

   > (1 + 4 + 9 + 16 + 25 + 36) = 91

   The program should receive input, display the input, display the Sum of the squares, and continue to receive input until the input is negative, in which the program terminates.

4. A metric ton is 35,273.92 ounces. Write a program that will read the weight of a package of candy in pounds and display the weight in metric tons.

5. Workers at a particular company have won a 5.6 % pay increase retroactive for six months. Write a program that takes an employee's previous annual salary as input, and displays the amount of retroactive pay due the employee, the new annual salary, and the new monthly salary. Your program should allow the calculation to be repeated until the user wishes to stop.

6. Write a program that asks the user to enter two numbers. The program should use the conditional operator to determine which number is the smaller and which is the larger.

7. Write a program that counts the number of its inputs that are positive, negative, and zero. Display the numbers and the counts.

8. Write a program that determines the number of strings and average string length in its input. Display the strings and the average string length.

9. Write a program to simulate a state police radar gun. The program should read an automobile speed and display the speed and a message if the speed exceeds 65 miles per hour.

10. Write a program that calculates and displays bills for the city water company. The water rates vary, depending on whether the bill is for home use, commercial use, and industrial use. A code h means home use, a code of c means commercial use, and a code of I means industrial use. Any other codes are errors and the program should display error messages. The water rate schedule is:

    Code h: $5.00 plus $0.0005 per gallon used

    Code c: $1000.00 for the first 4 million gallons used and $0.00025 for each additional gallon

    Code i: $1000.00 if usage does not exceed 4 million gallons; $2000.00 if the usage is more that 4 million gallons but does not exceed 10 million gallons; and $3000.00 if the usage exceeds 10 million gallons. Input is entered with an account number, bill code and the amount in gallons. The program calculates the water bill, displays all data read and the calculated bill. The program should terminate when the account number is negative.

11. Write a program that reads three nonzero double values and determines and displays the three values and if they could represent the sides of a rectangle.

12. Write a program that reads three nonzero integers and determines and displays the three values and if they could be the sides of a right triangle.

13. Write a program that sums a sequence of integers. Assume that the first integer read specifies the number of values remaining to be entered. Your program should read only one value per input statement. A typical input statement might be

   3 20 600 45

   where the 3 indicates that the subsequent 3 values are to be summed. Display the numbers read and the sum. The program should terminate when the number of values to read in a statement is negative.

14. Write a program that calculates and displays the odd integers and the product of the odd integers from 1 to 15.

4

Methods

4.1. Introduction

A **method** is a group of programming language statements that is given a name and other attributes. Every method in a Java program is part of a class. The code that defines the method is executed when it is call or invoked.

The flow of control is transferred to the entry point of a method after an invocation. Statements in the method are executed, one by one to an exit point in the method. Execution in the called method on exit from the calling method continues in the called method. A called method is part of the same or different class or object. If the called method is a part of the same class or object the invocation is made by use of the method name. If the called method is part of a different object the invocation is made through the object name.

4.2. Creating a Method

Methods are created with the following components:
- optional modifiers
- return type
- identifier
- parameters
- throws clause
- method body

Optional **modifiers** are keywords that determine whether the method is public or private. A **public method** is defined for use by every method in the object that contains the method and other methods that reference the object. **Private methods** are defined for use in the current object that contains the method. The **return type** follows the optional modifier. It indicates the type of value returned by the method when it is invoked. The return type may be void. An **identifier** is used to name the method. The name follows the return type. **Parameters** follow the method identifier and are used to transmit values to methods. Optional **throws clause** follows the parameters and are used to manage exceptions. Exceptions are discussed in Chapter 5. The **method body** is a block of statements that execute when the method is invoked. Method syntax is detailed in Figure 20.

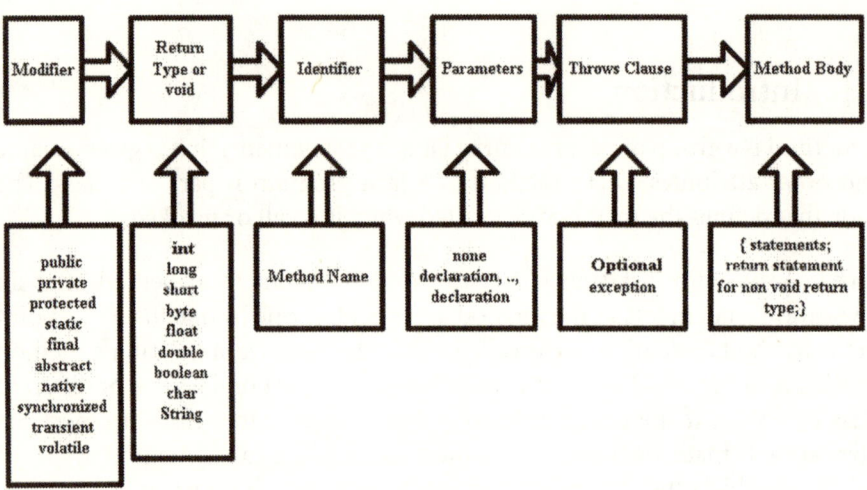

Figure 20. Method Syntax

For example, a method with a void return type is

```
public void for_print (int number, String message)
{
  int j;
  j = 0;
  do
  { System.out.println (message);
    // Increment the control-variable expression
    j = j + 1;
  } while (j < number);
}
```

For example, a method with an int return type is

```
public int number_loop (int number)
{
  int j;
  j = 0;
  do
  { System.out.println ("Hello Java");
    // Increment the control-variable expression
    j = j + 1;
  } while (j < number);
  return j;
}
```

For example, a method with an int return type and an empty parameter list is

```
public int count_loop ( )
{
  int j;
  j = 0;
  do
  { System.out.println ("Hello Java");
    // Increment the control-variable expression
    j = j + 1;
  } while (j < 50);
  return j;
}
```

A **parameter** is a value that is passed to a method when it is invoked. The parameter list is defined in the method header. The names of the parameters in the header of the method declaration are called **formal parameters.** Declared parameters in the parameter list are separated by a comma. Parameters declared in the method header may be referenced inside the method. A method definition with no parameter list declared is an empty set indicated with a set of parentheses.

A method with a return type returns a value and must contain a return statement. When a return statement is executed, control is immediately returned to the calling method. A return statement consists of the reserve word **return** followed by an expression consistent with the method return type.

4.3. Calling a Method

Values passed to a method in an invocation are called **actual parameters**. A method is called by use of its name.

For example, a code segment that calls the void method **for_print** in Section 4.2 is

```
int k = 20;
String myreport = "A Java Report";
for_print (k, myreport);
```

For example, a code segment that calls the int method **number_loop** in Section 4.2 is

```
int m;
int h = 40;
m = number_loop (h);
```

4.3.1. Passing Parameters

The calling method must pass actual parameters in the same order as their respective formal parameters in the called method specification.

For example, using parameter order association with the **for_print** method defined in Section 4.2 is

```
int k = 30;
String myreport = "Parameter Order Association";
for_print (k, myreport);
```

4.3.2. Pass by Value

When using primitive data types such as int the value of the actual parameter is passed to the called method. The value of the variable in the calling method is not changed after a return to the calling method.

4.4. Overloading Methods

Overloading involves using one term to indicate different meanings. Consider the use of the + sign in the code segment.

```
int x = 12;
int y = 30;
System.out.println ("This is a string " + x+y);
```

The output is This is a string 1230.
Change the output statement to

```
System.out.println (x+y + "This is a string");
```

The output is 42This is a string.

In this case the meaning of + is interpreted by the context of its use. When you overload a Java method, you write multiple methods with a shared name. The compiler interprets the meaning based on the arguments used with the method. For example, create a class method to calculate the distance given the rate in miles per hour and the time in hours. The method receives two double arguments, the rate and the time used to calculate the distance. Figure 21 details a method to calculate distance given the rate and time.

```
public static void distance (double rate, double time)
{ double calculate;
  calculate = rate * time;
  System.out.println ("The rate is " + rate + " and the time is " +
                      time + " Yields" + "a distance " + calculate);
}
```

Figure 21. Calculate Distance with Rate and Time in Hours

Suppose time is given in minutes. We desire to use the same method name to calculate the distance. **Overloading** involves writing multiple methods with the same name, but with different arguments. Figure 22 details a distance method with an integer argument for time.

```
public static void distance (double rate, integer time)
{
  double calculate;
  double hours;
  hours = time / 60;
  calculate = rate * hours;
  System.out.println ("The rate is " + rate + " and the time is " +
                      hours + " Yields" + "a distance " + calculate);
}
```

Figure 22. Calculate Distance with Rate ant Time in Minutes

The method in Figure 21 and Figure 22 name is distance. The compiler uses the method in a call based on the context of the method arguments.

```
double x = 10.0;     // miles per hour
double z = 32.0      // hours
distance (x, y);
```

The compiler executes the method defined in Figure 21 with two double arguments. Output generate is

The rate is 10.0 and the time is 32.0 Yields a distance 120.

```
double s = 10.0;     // miles per hour
int t = 120;         // minutes
distance (s, t);
```

The compiler executes the method defined in Figure 22 with one double and one integer argument. Output generate is

The rate is 10.0 and the time is 2.0 Yields a distance 20.

4.5. Creating Methods in Separate Classes

Thus far we have written methods in the same class as that in which they were invoked. Methods may be created in separate classes and used by other classes. Figure 23 details a class name **travel** to calculate distance given rate in miles per hour and time in hours.

```
  public class travel
  {
    public static void distance (double rate, double time)
    {
      double calculate;
      calculate = rate * time;
      System.out.println ("The rate is " + rate + " and the time is "
                          + time + " Yields" + " a distance " +
                          calculate);
    }
  }
  public class calculate
  {
    public static void main (String [ ] args)
    {
      double r = 45.0;    // miles per hour
      double t = 25.0;    // hours
      travel. distance (r, t);
    }
  }
```

Figure 23. Creating Methods in Separate Classes

The method **distance** is defined in the travel class. To invoke **distance**, put the class name **travel** followed by the character **dot** or period in front of the **distance** method name.

4.6. Method Abstraction

An **abstract method** is a method with no method statements. Define an abstract method with the keyword abstract followed by the intended method type, name, and arguments with no statements within the method. When you create a subclass that inherits an abstract method from a parent, you must provide the actions, or implementation, for the inherited method. A subclass method to override the empty superclass method that is inherited must be coded.

For example, create classes to represent different toys, such as trucks and cars. Create a generic abstract class named **toys** that provides generic data fields, such as the toy's name, only once. A toy is generic, but all specific toys make a sound. The actual sound differs from toy to toy. Code an empty **sound ( )**

method in the abstract toy class. Code is required for all future toy subclasses for a **sound ( )** method that is specific to the subclass. Figure 24 details an abstract toy class containing a data field for the name, a constructor, a **getName ( )** method, and an abstract **sound ( )** method.

```
public abstract class toy
{
  private String name;
  public toy (String nam)// class constructor
  {
    name = nam;
  }
  public String getName ( )   // concrete method
  {
    return name;
  }
  public abstract void sound ( );  // abstract method
}
```

Figure 24. Toy Class

Since the toy class contain the abstract method **sound ( )** it must be defined as an abstract class. Class constructors are defined in Chapter 7.

An abstract class like toy may be created so that it is extended. For example, a truck is a toy, create a truck class as a child class of toy. Figure 25 details a truck class that extends toy. The toy class in Figure 24 contains a constructor that requires a String holding the toy's name, so the child truck class also must contain a constructor that passes a String along to its superclass constructor.

```
public class truck extends toy
{
  public truck (String nam)
  {
    super (nam);
  }
  public void sound ( )
  {
    System.out.println ("Mack");
  }
}
```

Figure 25. Truck Class

The class in Figure 26 inherit from the toy class. When you create a car the toy will be able to use sound ( ).

```
public class car extends toy
{
  public truck (String nam)
  {
    super (nam)
  }
  public void sound ( )
  {
    System.out.println ("Toyota");
  }
}
```

Figure 26. Car Class

4.7. Recursion

In Java, any method can call another method. When a method calls itself, it is making a recursive call. Recursion is a powerful technique that can be used in place of iteration or looping.

An operation is said to be defined recursively if its definition consists of two parts:

1. An anchor or **base case**, in which the value produced by the operation is specified for one or more values of the operands.
2. An inductive or **recursive step**, in which the value produced for current value of the operands is defined in terms of previously defined results and/or operand values.

Figure 27 details a Java method name **sumoffirst** that computes and returns the sum of the first n integers.

```
public int sumoffirst (int n)
{ if (n == 1)
  {
    return 1;                          // The base case
  }
  else
  {
    int smallsum = sumoffirst (n - 1);
    // Call the general case with a smaller problem.
    return smallsum + n;
    // Compute and return the next larger sum.
  }
}
```

Figure 27. Compute and Return the Sum of the First n Integers

For example, calculating sumoffirst (4):

```
sumoffirst (4)  = 4 + sumoffirst (3)
                = 4 + 3 + sumoffirst (2)
                = 4 + 3 + 2 + sumoffirst (1)
                = 4 + 3 + 2 + 1
```

4.8. Recursion versus Iteration

Recursion is repetitive execution without a loop control in which successive recursive calls are handled behind the scenes by the system. An **iteration** process is a specified loop body controlled by a loop control structure.

Recursion uses more overhead that is managed by the system. Each time the program calls a method, the system must assign space for all of the local variables and parameters of the method. If you are concerned about performance of your program, avoid using recursion because it takes more time and consumes more memory than iteration. Some classical recursive algorithms perform best when implemented with recursive programs.

4.9. Exercises

All components of applications must be implemented using methods.

1. Create an application **myrecord** with fields that hold a patient number, two blood pressure figures called systolic and diastolic, and two cholesterol figures called LDL and HDL. Include methods to get and set each of the fields. Include a method named **ratio ( )** that divides LDL cholesterol by HDL cholesterol and display the results. Include a method named **eval_cholest ( )** that explains that LDL is known as good and that a ratio of 3.5 or lower is cholesterol optimum.

2. Write a Java program to determine the answers for each of the following:
    1. The square root of 45
    2. The sin and cosine of 100
    3. The value of the floor, ceiling, and round of 66.9
    4. The larger and the smaller of the character K and the integer 70

3. Write a program to calculate how many days it is from today until the end of the current year.

4. The formula for converting from Fahrenheit to Celsius is

    Fahrenheit = 1.8 * Celsius + 32

    Write an application with methods that read a temperature and use methods that compute Celsius to Fahrenheit and Fahrenheit to Celsius. Display the input and the conversions.

5. Write a recursive method that will compute factorials. The factorial of a natural number is defined as

    factorial (0) = 1;
    factorial (n) = factorial (n - 1) x n; for n > 0

    The program reads a number n, computes the factorial, and displays the number and the factorial.

6. Write a program to display the square root of floating point numbers counting by 2's from 0 to 24.

5

Exception Handling

5.1. Introduction

An **exception** is an unexpected or error condition that occurs during the program's execution. Programs can generate many types of exceptions, such as:

- Read a file from disk that does not exist.
- Write a file to an unformatted disk.
- A user enters invalid data as input to a program.
- The program attempts to divide a value by zero.

These errors are called exceptions because the conditions are not normal. Java provides the capability to let the programmer handle runtime errors under program control. The object-oriented techniques used to manage errors under program control are a group of methods called **exception handling**.

In Java programming, exceptions are Objects and the class name is Exception. Basic classes of error in a Java program are **Error** and **Exception**. These classes descend from the **Throwable** class. The Error class is used to manage errors from which your program cannot recover. For example, when you spell a class name incorrectly or store a required class in the wrong folder.

5.2. Exceptions and Exception Types

A Java exception is an instance of a class derived from **Throwable**. Class **Throwable** is contained in the **java.lang** package. Subclasses of Throwable are contained in other packages. Exception classes are created by extending class Throwabe or a subclass of Throwable.

Class Exception is a subclass of class Throwable. The Exception class contains less serious errors that are recoverable under user program control. There are many classes that inherit class Exception. These subclasses are stored in many packages. For example, some Exception subclasses are: **RuntimeException, IOException, ArrayIndexOutOfBoundsException, TooManyListenersException,** and **ArithmeticException.**

Class **Error** is a subclass of class **Throwable**. The **Error** class contains serious errors that are unrecoverable under user program control. Many classes are inherited from class Errors. For example, come Error subclasses are: **OutOfMemoryException, InternalErrorException,** and **LinkageError.**

5.3. Understanding Exception Handling

The Java exception model is based on three exception operations: claiming, throwing, and catching.

Every Java statement in a Java program is a member of a method **main ( )** or a method that is invoked by another method. Every method must state the type of exceptions it can check. This process is called **claiming an exception** that indicates what can go wrong.

A statement causes errors in a program defined to claim an exception. A method containing the statement creates an exception object and passes it to the system. The exception object contains information about the exception such as its type and the state of the program. The process of interpreting the error is called **throwing an exception.**

A method is defined to throw an exception. After a method throws an exception, the Java runtime system starts the process to find the code to handle the exception. Code that handles exceptions is called the **exception handler.** The exception handler for a code segment is found by backward chaining through the method calls starting from the current method. If no handler is found the program terminates; otherwise, the handler is executed. The process of finding a handler is called **catching an exception.**

5.3.1. Claiming Exceptions

Claim an exception by telling the compiler what may go wrong while executing a method. Java does not require you to claim Error and RuntimeException in the method. The programmer must act to make the compiler aware of other exceptions that must be claimed in the declaration of the method. Use the throws keyword in the **first** method declaration to claim an **IOException** as:

```
public void first ( ) throws IOException
```

5.3.2. Throwing Exceptions

In a method that claimed an exception, you can throw an object of the exception if the exception arises. For, example the syntax to throw an exception is:

```
throw new TheException ( );
```

or

```
TheException b = new TheException ( ); throw b;
```

Figure 28 details a **ratio** method that throws an exception when a divide-by-zero error is encountered.

```
// ratio method
// Uses throwing exception when a divide-by-zero error is encountered.
   public  double ratio (int numer, int denom)
          throws dividebz
{
  if (denom == 0)
    throw new dividebz ( );
  // Make the calculation and return the quitient.
  return (double) numer / denom);
  }
// Class definition for dividebz
public  class dividebz
        extends ArithmeticException
{
  public dividebz ( )
  {
    super ("Division by zero is not allowed.");
  }
```

```
    public dividebz (String message)
    {
      super (message);
    }
  } // End dividezb class
```

Figure 28. Throws Exception

5.3.3. Trying and Catching Exceptions

When you have a code segment in which something can go wrong, place the code in a **try block**. A try block is not a class and the code segment consists of elements:

Description	Program Statements
The keyword try	try
An opening curly bracket	{
Statements that may cause Exceptions	statement (s);
A closing curly bracket	}

At least one catch block must immediately follow a try block. A code segment that takes action to deal with an error condition is a **catch block**. Each catch block can "catch" one type of Exception. A catch block is not a class and the code segment consists of elements:

Description	Program Statements
The keyword catch	catch
An opening parenthesis	(
An Exception type	someException
A name for an instance of the Exception	nameExceptionInstance
A closing parenthesis	)
An opening curly bracket	{
Statements that take actions for the error	statement (s);
A closing curly bracket	}

Actions to perform at the end of a try catch sequence are placed in a **finally block**. The code in a **finally block** executes whether or not the try block identifies Exceptions. A finally block is not a class and the code segment consists of elements:

Description	Program Statements
A keyword	finally
An open curly bracket	{
Statements to execute even if no Exception	statement (s);
A closing curly bracket	}

5.4. Exercises

1. Write a program that throws and catches an ArithmetricException. Declare a variable and assign it a value. Test the variable, and if it is negative, throw an ArithmeticException. Otherwise use the Math.sqrt ( ) method to determine the square root.

2. Write a program that displays a student number and ask the user to enter a numeric test score for the student. Create a **score** exception class, and throw a **score** exception for that class if the user does not enter a valid score less than or equal to 100. Catch the **score** exception and then display a message.

3. Write a program that read an ID number and an age. Create an Exception class and throw an Exception of that class if the ID is not in the range of valid ID numbers zero through 899, or if the age is not in the range of valid ages 0 through 89. Catch the Exception and then display a message.

4. Write a Java program that determines how various exceptions are cought with

    catch (Exception e)

6
File Input and Output

6.1. Introduction

Data are organized as fields and records are called a **file**. Files are stored as none volatile data on secondary storage. The devices that manipulate secondary storage are called **secondary storage devices**. Computer systems use file systems to organize the secondary storage using files and directories. A **directory** is a mechanism for cataloging that is organized in a tree structure. Directories are managed by the system operating system. A set of files can be grouped together into a single directory that facilitates easy access. Another name for directory is a **folder**. Files are located in a file system by finding a direct path from the root of the tree to the folder that contains the file. For example, a file name **mydata.dat** is stored on a hard disk whose logical device name is "c" in a folder called **car** that is a subdirectory of a root directory **auto**. The directed path to the file **mydata.dat** is:

    c:\auto\car\mydata.dat

In most cases, the direct path is used as a String in Java. Remember that the back slash (\) is part of the set of characters that define control sequences. When initializing a string with back slash use two back slashes to let Java know that you are not defining a control sequence. The direct path in a string **fname** is:

```
String fname = "c:\\auto\\car\\mydata.dat"
```

6.2. File Classes

Java views file data as a stream of bytes. A stream of bytes from which data are read is called an **input stream**. A stream of bytes that are written is called an **output stream**. Java provides classes for connecting and manipulating data in a stream in the **java.io** package. Some selected classes used for input and output are detailed in Figure 29.

Class	Description
InputStreamReader on FileInputStream	Read one character at a time from a text file.
BufferedReader on InputStreamReader FileInputStream	Read one line at a time from a text file.
StreamTokenizer on BufferedReader on InputStreamReader on FileInputStream	Read one word at a time from a text file.
PrintWriter on FileOutputStream	Write int, double, char, String,…to a text file.
DataOutputStream on FileOutputStream	Write int, double, char, String,…to a non-text file.
DataInputStream on FileInputStream	Read int, double, char, String,…from a non-text file.
ObjectOutputStream on FileOutputStream	Write an object to a file.
ObjectInputStream on FileInputStream	Read an object from a file.
System.in which is a BufferedReader on InputStreamReader on InputStream	Read keyboard input.
System.out and System.err which are PrintStream objects	Write console output.

Figure 29. Selected Input and Output Classes

6.3. File and Dialog Objects

Some implementations require the user to interact with a GUI dialog to open existing files and save into files. We can use a **FileDialog** object from the **java.awt** package to select a file or a directory. You can open the object in the **Load mode** if you want to read data from the selected file and in the **Save mode** if you want to write data to the selected file. For example, the statements to **Open** a file is:

```
FileDialog filebox = new FileDialog (mainWindow, "Open",
                                     FileDialog.LOAD);
filebox.setVisible (true);
```

The user can browse the directories and select the desired file by clicking on the filename in the file list or typing the filename in the File name: text field. The selected file is retrieved with the **getFile** ( ) method from a visible dialog. The statement is:

```
String myname = filebox.getFile ( );
```

The selected file name is assigned to the string variable **myname**. If the Cancel button or the Open button without a file name of FileDialog is clicked, then the getFile ( ) method returns a null.

The path name to the directory where the selected file is located obtained with:

```
File infile = new File (directoryPath, myname);
```

To select a file for saving data open the FileDialog in the **Save mode:**

```
FileDialog filebox = new FileDialog (mainWindow, "Save As",
                                     FileDialog.SAVE);
filebox.setVisible (true);
```

6.4. Keyboard Input

Input on the keyboard is accomplished by defining an **InputStreamReader**. The **BufferedReader** class is used to create a single shared reader for keyboard input. Create a single shared BufferedReader for keyboard input as:

```
private static BufferedReader stdin = new BufferedReader (new
InputStreamReader(System.in));
```

Throw an **IOException** on the **main** ( ) method as:

```
public static void main (String arg [ ]) throws IOException
```

Read from the keyboard with

```
String input = stdin.readLine ( );
```

Steps that implement a keyboard input using BufferedReader are:

1. Define the Java class head **keyin** that include import packages and variable declarations.

   ```
   import java.io.*;
   public class keyin         /* Class Head */
   { // Global variables defined in the head of the class block
     private static int sand;
   ```

2. You plan to read from the key board. Define a Java reader to manage input from the keyboard to your Java program. Create a single shared BufferedReader for keyboard input.

   ```
   private static BufferedReader stdin = new BufferedReader (new
   InputStreamReader(System.in));
   ```

3. Define the head of the unique main Java method with variable declarations.

   ```
   public static void main (String arg [ ])
       throws IOException
   { // Local variables defined in the head of the main method block
     int number;

     // Assign class variable value
     sand = 10;
   ```

4. Input the number of cars and trucks using the BufferedReader for keyboard input. The input is a string stored in a variable called **input**.

   ```
   System.out.println("Keyboard Input");
   System.out.println(" ");
   // Input the test number
   System.out.println ("Type the test number and press enter ");
   String input = stdin.readLine ( );
   ```

5. Convert the String received from the keyboard to an integer. Store the integer in a variable called **number**.

   ```
   number = Integer.parseInt (input);
   ```

6. Print the results on the console.

   ```
   sand = sand + number;
   // Print the test number
   System.out.println ("The test number is: " + number);
   // Print the calculated sum
   System.out.println ("The calculated sum is " + sand);
   ```

7. Define the tail of the Java main method.

   ```
   } // End of Java main method
   ```

8. Define the tail of the Java class keyin.

   ```
   } // Class tail or end of Java class keyin
   ```

A keyboard example is detailed in the **keyin class** which must be named **keyin.java**.

```
import java.io.*;
public class keyin /* Class Head */
{ // Global variables defined in the head of the class block
  private static int sand;

  // Create a single shared BufferedReader for keyboard input
  private static BufferedReader stdin = new BufferedReader (new
  InputStreamReader(System.in));

  // The main Java Method
  public static void main (String arg [ ])
     throws IOException
  { // Local variables defined in the head of the main method block
    int number;

    // Assign class variable value
    sand = 10;

    System.out.println("Keyboard Input");
    System.out.println(" ");
    // Input the test number
    System.out.println ("Type the test number and press enter ");
    String input = stdin.readLine ( );
    // Convert string input to an integer
    number = Integer.parseInt (input);
    sand = sand + number;
```

```
        // Print the test number
        System.out.println ("The test number is: " + number);
        // Print the calculated sum
        System.out.println ("The calculated sum is " + sand);
    } // End of Java main method
} // Class tail or end of Java class keyin
```

A screen view of the keyin class execution with input 350 is:

```
C:\j2sdk1.4.2_04\bin\java.exe - Finished
Keyboard Input

Type the test number and press enter
350
The test number is:   350
The calculated sum is   360
```

6.5. File Input

Reading from a text file can be accomplished in many ways. One way to read from a text file is one character at a time. Another way to read text from a file is a line or record from the file in one method call. The **BufferedReader** class provides the capability to read a file one character at a time and one line with one method call. For example, an application called **iobuf** with implementation steps is detailed in Figure 30.

Implementation steps for a class that reads text data from a file using BufferedReader are:

1. Define the Java class head **iobuf** that include import packages and variable declarations.

    ```
    import javax.swing.*;
    import java.io.*;
    class iobuf
    {
    ```

2. Define a Java reader to manage input from a file. Setup the FileReader in a method called ibuf. The method ibuf uses a Java type modifier called BufferedReader. A BufferedReader pointer is returned that defines a Reader for the input file on a storage device.

```
    private BufferedReader ibuf (String filename)
    throws java.io.IOException
    {
      // Set up the basic input stream
      FileReader fr = new FileReader (filename);
      // Buffer the input stream
      BufferedReader br = new BufferedReader (fr);
      return br;
    } // End ibuf Method
```

3. Define a method called inf that reads a line of data from the input file. The method inf has a Java type modifier of String. A string is returned of the data read. The BufferedReader pointer is managed automatically by the system. This pointer should not be managed by the programmer unless detailed experience has been acquired.

```
    //----------------------------------------
    // Input a Data Item
    //----------------------------------------
    public static String inf (BufferedReader br)
    throws java.io.IOException
    { String inval;
      if ((inval = br.readLine ( )) != null)
        {
          return inval;
        } else return null;
    } // End inf Method
```

4. Define the head of the unique main Java method with variable declarations.

```
    public static void main (String args[ ])
    throws java.io.IOException
    { // Delcare Variables
      String sentinel = "AA";
      int Total = 0;
```

5. Instantiate an object iobuf with a container reference DL.

```
      iobuf DL = new iobuf ( );
```

6. Define a BufferedReader variable.

```
      BufferedReader tk;
```

7. Setup a path to the input file name.

   ```
   String fname = "C:\\session\\data\\INFO.DAT";
   ```

8. Point the BufferedReader variable at the file name.

   ```
   tk = DL.ibuf (fname);
   ```

9. Define the head of a while loop to read an input data items one-at-a-time using the inf method. The BufferedReader pointer is positioned automatically to the next record after each **inf** method call.

   ```
   System.out.println("Storage Device Input");
   System.out.println(" ");
   while (sentinel != null)
   { // Input Data and Return String Data Value
     sentinel = DL.inf (tk);
   ```

10. Convert the String read from the storage device to an integer and add it to the variable Total.

    ```
    // Add to Total
    if (sentinel != null) Total = Total +
                                  Integer.parseInt (sentinel);
    ```

11. Display the results in a GUI dialog box.

    ```
    // Post GUI With Data
    JOptionPane.showMessageDialog (null, "Value = " + sentinel);
    } // End while

    // Post Total Value
    JOptionPane.showMessageDialog(null, "Total of all Information = "
                                  + Total);

    // Close the Input File
    tk.close ( );

    // Terminate Program
    System.exit (0);
    ```

12. Define the tail of the Java main method.

    ```
    } // End main Method
    ```

13. Define the tail of the Java class iobuf.

```
} // End iobuf class
```

An iobuf class that is stored with a file name **iobuf.java**.

```
import javax.swing.*;
import java.io.*;
class iobuf
{
  //----------------------------------------
  // Setup File Reference Handle
  //----------------------------------------
  private BufferedReader ibuf (String filename)
  throws java.io.IOException
  {
    // Set up the basic input stream
    FileReader fr = new FileReader (filename);
    // Buffer the input stream
    BufferedReader br = new BufferedReader (fr);
    return br;
  } // End ibuf Method

  //----------------------------------------
  // Input a Data Item
  //----------------------------------------
  public static String inf (BufferedReader br)
  throws java.io.IOException
  { String inval;
    if ((inval = br.readLine ( )) != null)
      {
        return inval;
      } else return null;
  } // End inf Method

  public static void main (String args[ ])
  throws java.io.IOException
  { // Delcare Variables
    String sentinel = "AA";
    int Total = 0;
    // Define a Reference Variable to the Container
    iobuf DL = new iobuf ( );
    BufferedReader tk;
    // Set the Path and Input File Name
    String fname = "C:\\session\\data\\INFO.DAT";
```

```
    // Setup file reference handle
    tk = DL.ibuf (fname);
    System.out.println("Storage Device Input");
    System.out.println(" ");

    // Read an Input Data Items One-at-a-Time
    while (sentinel != null)
    { // Input Data and Return String Data Value
      sentinel = DL.inf (tk);
      // Add to Total
      if (sentinel != null) Total = Total +
                                    Integer.parseInt (sentinel);

      // Post GUI With Data
      JOptionPane.showMessageDialog (null, "Value = " + sentinel);
    } // End while

    // Post Total Value
    JOptionPane.showMessageDialog(null, "Total of all Information = "
                                    + Total);

    // Close the Input File
    tk.close ( );

    // Terminate Program
    System.exit (0);
  } // End main Method
} // End iobuf class
```

Figure 30. Read a Text File with BufferReader

The **ibuf** method receives a text path with a text file name as an actual parameter. **BufferedReader** allocates a reference variable and associates it with the file name. A **BufferedReader** reference pointer is returned. The **inf** method receives a **BufferedReader** reference pointer as an actual parameter. One text item read from the text file is returned as a string of one character. The **main ( )** method allocates an object with a reference variable **DL**, defines a **BufferedReader** variable **tk**, initializes a string **fname** to the path and text file name, allocates a **BufferedReader** reference variable associated with **fname**, and setup a while loop to invoke **inf** with the **BufferedReader** reference variable as an actual parameter to read the text file data.

The iobuf class was executed with an input file that contained numbers 40 and 56. The program displayed each number read in a dialog box.

The first number read.

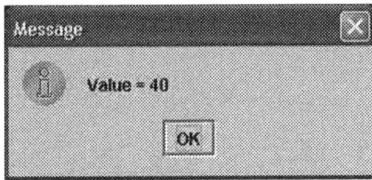

The second number read.

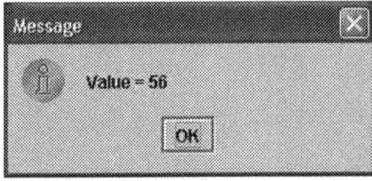

Total of numbers read.

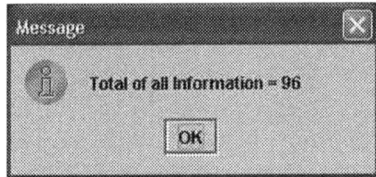

6.6. File Output

Java has many ways to write data in files. In this section, we declare our own stream of characters as an output file and write information to it. We must carry out steps:

1. Create a stream object and associate it with a disk file.
2. Give the stream object the desired functionality.
3. Read information from an input file or write information to an output file.
4. Close the file.

Figure 31. Allocate a File and Write Information

The output file name is **outtext.txt**. Declare **outstream** as a new object of type **FileWriter** and associate it with the disk file named **outtext.txt** in the current directory.

```
FileWriter outstream = new FileWriter ("outtext.txt");
```

A **FileWriter** object only write strings, characters, and integer values to an output stream using method **write** ( ). Wrap outstream in a new object **outtxt**, which has methods **print** ( ) and **println** ( ) for writing String objects and all primitive data types.

```
PrintWriter outtxt - new PrintWriter (outstream);
```

Steps 1 and 2 from Figure 31 are satisfied.

Use Java statements to define the core of the application. At the end of the program close the output file **outtext.txt**.

```
outtxt.close ( );
```

Implementation steps for a tfo class to write a text file on a storage device:

1. Define the Java class head **tfo** that include import packages and variable declarations. The **class tfo** writes text to an output stream.

    ```
    import java.io.*;
    public class tfo
    {
    ```

2. Define the head of the unique main Java method with variable declarations.

    ```
    public static void main (String args [ ]) throws IOException
    {
    ```

3. Define a **try** after the exception has been thrown.

    ```
    try
    {
    ```

4. Allocate a **FileWriter** object **outstream** for an output file outtext.txt.

    ```
    FileWriter outstream = new FileWriter ("outtext.txt");
    ```

5. Wrap the **FileWriter** object outstream with a **PrintWriter** object **outtxt**.

    ```
    PrintWriter outtxt = new PrintWriter (outstream);
    ```

6. Write output to the file **outtext.txt** with **println** a member of the **PrintWriter class.**

    ```
    System.out.println("Write Text to a Storage Device");
    System.out.println(" ");
    outtxt.println ("My first output is 80");
    outtxt.println ("Your number is 20");
    outtxt.println ("Rule is 80");
    ```

7. Write a message to the console.

    ```
    System.out.println ("File written to the output device.");
    ```

8. Close the output file **outtext.txt**.

    ```
    outtxt.close ( );
    ```

9. Close the try block.

    ```
    } // End of try Block
    ```

10. Define the head of a catch block for the try block. Every try must have at least one catch block.

    ```
    catch (IOException b)
    {
    ```

11. If an IOException occurs the catch block is executed. The statements in the catch block are executed.

    ```
    System.out.println ("I/O error: " + b.getMessage ( ));
    ```

12. Define the tail of the catch block.

    ```
    } // End of catch Block
    ```

13. Define the tail of the Java main method.

    ```
    } // End main Method
    ```

14. Define the tail of the Java **class tfo**.

```
} // End tfo Class
```

A application in Figure 32 details the writing of text data to an output file **outtext.txt**. The class tfo is stored with the file name **tfo.java**.

```
// Write text to an output stream.
import java.io.*;
public class tfo
{
  public static void main (String args [ ]) throws IOException
  {
    try
    {
      FileWriter outstream = new FileWriter ("outtext.txt");
      PrintWriter outtxt = new PrintWriter (outstream);
      System.out.println("Write Text to a Storage Device");
      System.out.println(" ");

      // Write three lines to the output file outtext.txt
      outtxt.println ("My first output is 80");
      outtxt.println ("Your number is 20");
      outtxt.println ("Rule is 80");

      // Write a console message
      System.out.println ("File written to the output device.");

      // Close the output file outtext.txt.
      outtxt.close ( );
    } // End of try Block
    catch (IOException b)
    {
      System.out.println ("I/O error: " + b.getMessage ( ));
    } // End of catch Block
  } // End main Method
} // End tfo Class
```

Figure 32. Wite a Text Output File

6.7. Exercises

1. Write a program that will count the number of characters, words, and lines in a file. The file name should be passed as a command-line argument.

2. Write a program that prompts the user for a file name and then outputs whether a file of that name exists in the current directory. If it exists in the current directory display:

    Whether the file can be read from or written to.
    What the file length is.

3. Using the try-catch block, write code that opens a file **henry.dat** when an attempt to open a user-designated file raises an exception.

4. Write a program that reads names from a text file. The names are separated by new-line characters, are in sorted order, and some are duplicated names. The program should write the names to a different text file without the duplicated names. Allow the user to specify the file names.

7
Object-Oriented Programming

Java is a pure object-oriented language. All methods are part of a class with no multiple inheritance. Formal interface specifications are available with no parameterized type and no operator overloading. All methods except final methods are dynamically bound.

7.1. Introduction

Object-oriented programming (OOP) organizes programs in a way that models real-life objects. In Java a program is viewed as a collection of cooperating objects using abstraction, encapsulation, reusability, and inheritance. The fundamentals of object-oriented programming are declaring classes, creating objects, manipulating objects, and making objects working together.

Object-oriented programming allows programmers to create a new class from an existing class. The new class extends an existing base class. The new class inherits data and methods from the base class. Additional methods may be added to the base class by inheritance or existing methods can be changed or overridden.

Java has a library of classes that can be used. This provides a means for programmers to reuse classes. Programs can be made from off-the-shelf components that enhance program development. Java libraries may be accessed with the import statement.

7.2. Objects and Classes

An **object** is a set of data and the methods which operate on the data. A set of properties define an object, and behaviors define the object actions. Properties are known as data fields, and the objects' behaviors are defined by methods. Figure 33 details an object with its data fields and methods.

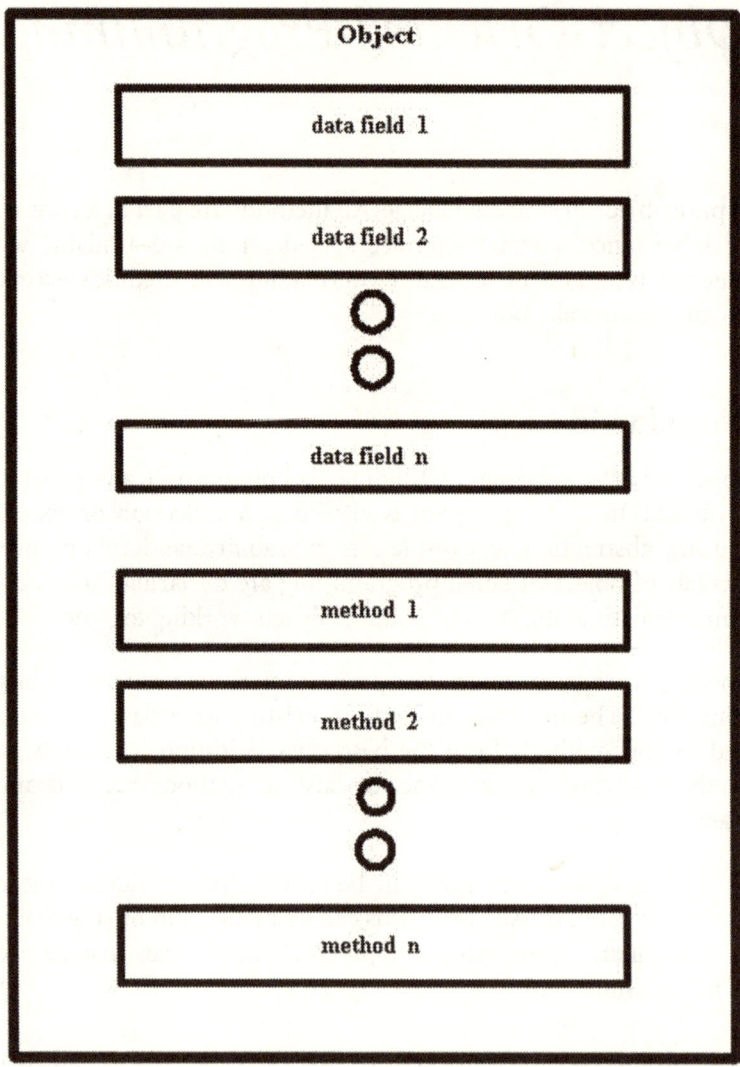

Figure 33. Object with Data Fields and Methods

For example, a quadratic object has data fields for the coefficients, which are the properties that characterize a quadratic. One behavior of a quadratic is that its range values can be computed from its domain values.

A **class** is a template for creating objects. Java class must be stored with a file name that is the same name and font size as the class name with an extension of .java. A class called quadratic is stored as **quadratic.java** on a storage device.

The following is an example of a class for a quadratic:

```
public class quadratic     // class head
{ // begin class body
   double a = 1.0;         // data field
   double b = 5.0;         // data field
   double c = 6.0;         // data field
   double evaluate (double x) // method for a quadratic calculation
   {return a * x * x + b * x + c;}
} // end class body
```

The code for the quadratic class is a definition that is used to declare and create quadratic objects. This class does not have a **main ( )** method, nor does it extend **java.applet.JApplet**. Applets will be discussed in Chapter 10. The class that contains the **main ( )** method is called the main class.

7.2.1. Declaring and Creating Objects

An **object** is an instance of a class. An object is composed of values, called instance variables, and operations that it can perform on those values, called instance methods. Creating an instance is referred to as instantiation. A declaration statement is used to declare an object and represent it with a class variable. The syntax for declaring a class variable is:

```
classname objectname;
```

Declare a variable **quad_value** to be an instance of the quadratic class.

```
quadratic quad_value;
```

A declaration does not create an object. An object is created for **quad_value** by using the new operator to allocating memory space for it. The syntax for creating an object is:

```
objectname = new classname ( );
```

The statement that creates an object **quad_value** and allocates memory space for quad_value is:

```
quad_value = new quadratic ( );
```

The combine declaration and instantiation syntax is:

```
classname objectname = new classname ( );
```

For example, create and instantiate **quad_value** in one step as:

```
quadratic quad_value = new quadratic ( );
```

Primitive data types may be converted to objects. For example, convert the data declared as int to an integer object.

```
int book = 50;                          // integer data
Integer obook = new Integer (book);     // integer object
```

7.2.2. Constructors

Object members may be initialized when it is created by a constructor method. A **constructor** is a method with the same name as the class. The programmer provides the constructor. If no explicit constructor is defined by the programmer a default constructor is defined by the Java compiler. The constructor is invoked automatically each time an object of the class is instantiated. Instance variables can be initialized implicitly to their default values, can be initialized in a constructor of the class, or their values may be set later after the object is created. Constructors cannot specify return types or return values. A class may contain overloaded constructors to provide a variety of means for initializing objects of that class.

When an object of a class is created, initializers can be provided in parenthesis to the right of the class name. The initializers are passed as arguments to the class's constructor. For example, constructors with arguments are:

```
classname objectname = new classname (arguments);
```

classname objectname is the appropriate data type, new indicates that a new object is being created, **classname** indicates the type of the object and arguments specifies the values used by the class's constructor to initialize the object. A **quadratic** class in Figure 34 details explicit constructors.

```
public class quadratic // class head
{ // begin class body
   private double a = 0.0; // data field
   private double b = 0.0; // data field
   private double c = 0.0; // data field
   public quadratic ( ) // constructor
   { a = 1.0;
     b = 5.0;
     c = 6.0;
   }
   public quadratic (double myvalue) // constructor
   { a = myvalue;
     b = 9.0;
     c = 18.0;
   }
   public double evaluate (double x) // method for a quadratic calculation
   { return a * x * x + b * x + c; }
   public double linear_only (double x) // method for a linear calculation
   { return b * x + c; }
} // end class body
```

Figure 34. Quadratic Class with Explicit Constructors

7.2.3. Modifiers

Modifiers are used in Java to control access to data, methods, and classes. Frequently used modifiers are static, public, protected, and private.

Static defines data and methods. Static data and methods are shared by all instances of the class. Public defines classes, methods, and data that can be accessed by all programs. Protected defines methods and data in such a way that any class in the same package or any subclasses of that class can access them, even if the class is in a different package. Private defines methods and data in such a way that they can be accessed by the declaring class, but not by the subclasses.

These modifiers apply to variables or to methods. If public, private, or protected is not used, by default, the classes, methods, and data are accessible by any class in the same package. Information on packages is detailed in Section 7.7.

7.3. Passing Objects to Methods

Values of variables may be passed to methods. Objects may be passed to methods as actual parameters. For example, the **quad_linear** object is passed to method linear.

```
class pass_object
{ public static void main (String [ ] args)
  { quadratic quad_linear = new quadratic (0.0);
    linear (quad_linear);
  }

  public static void linear (quadratic q)
  { System.out.println ("The linear value is " + q.evaluate (3.0));
  }
}
```

The reference of the object is passed to the method as a formal parameter. Since the reference to the object is passed, any changes to the object in the method body will affect the original object.

7.4. Instance Variables and Class Variables

Instance variables belong to each instance of the class. Instance variables are not shared among objects of the same class. Create objects **quad_value** and **linear_value**.

```
quadratic quad_value = new quadratic ( );
quadratic linear_value = new quadratic (0.0);
```

The objects **quad_value** and **linear_value** have independent data, and is in different memory locations.

Class variables may be shared. Class variables store values for the variables in a common memory location. Declare the class variables as static to share common data.

7.5. Instance Methods and Class Methods

Instance methods can be applied after the instances are created. They are applied with a call with the instance variable or reference to the object.

```
objectname.methodname ( );
```

The methods defined in the quadratic class in Figure 34 are instance methods. Static class methods can be called without creating an instance of the class. Declare the static method as:

```
static returntype staticmethod ( );
```

The **println** ( ) method in the System class is an example of a class method. The syntax of another way to call a class method is:

```
classname.methodname ( );
```

7.6. The Scope of Variables

The **scope of a variable** is the block in which it is declared. In the case of nested blocks, a variable declared in an outer block is accessible in any inner block. Variables declared inside a block will not be accessible outside the block. The same variable cannot be declared in nested blocks inside a method.

7.7. Packages

A **package** is a collection of classes. It provides a way to organize classes in libraries. Packages provide a mechanism for software reuse. Another benefit of packages is that they provide a convention for unique class names.

The steps for creating a reusable class are:
1. Define a public class. Public classes can be used by classes in other packages. Non-public classes can be used only by other classes in the same class.
2. Choose a package name and add a package statement to the source code file for reusable class definition.
3. Compile the class to place it in the package directory structure and make it available to the compiler and the interpreter.
4. Import the reusable class into a program and use the class.

Packages are stored in directories to keep them organized. Directories on a computer system may be nested to many levels. The java package statement uses the directory path to store packages. Directory paths are separated with a "dot" or period for each level of the directory. For example, a directory **first** with a subdirectory **goal** is represented as **first.goal**. If the first directory is located in the root of the c-drive the path is **c:\first\goal**. Class source code example with the package statement is detailed in Figure 35.

Create a Java class quadratic and store it in a package name **first.goal**.

1. Create a package called **first.goal**.

   ```
   package first.goal;
   ```

2. Define the head of a quadratic class including package imports and class variable declarations.

   ```
   import java.io.*;
   public class quadratic         // class head
   { // begin class body
       private double a = 0.0;    // data field
       private double b = 0.0;    // data field
       private double c = 0.0;    // data field
   ```

3. Define a quadratic constructor. The constructor has the same as the class with no Java method type modifier.

   ```
       public quadratic ( )       // constructor
       { a = 1.0;
         b = 5.0;
         c = 6.0;
       }
   ```

4. Defile a second quadratic constructor. The constructor name is quadratic with no Java method type modifier. This constructor has a formal parameter.

   ```
       public quadratic (double myvalue) // constructor
       { a = myvalue;
         b = 9.0;
         c = 18.0;
       }
   ```

5. Calculate the range of a quadratic with the method called evaluate. The Java method type modifier for evaluate is double.

   ```
   public double evaluate (double x)
   { return a * x * x + b * x + c; }
   ```

6. Calculate the range of a linear function with the method linear_only. The Java method type modifier for linear is double.

   ```
   public double linear_only (double x)
   { return b * x + c; }
   ```

7. Define the tail of the quadratic class.

   ```
   } // End quadratic class body
   ```

Implemented application using a package statement with a class that is saved in a file called **quadratic.java**.

```
package first.goal;
public class quadratic         // class head
{ // begin class body
  private double a = 0.0;      // data field
  private double b = 0.0;      // data field
  private double c = 0.0;      // data field
  public quadratic ( )         // constructor
  { a = 1.0;
    b = 5.0;
    c = 6.0;
  }
  public quadratic (double myvalue) // constructor
  { a = myvalue;
    b = 9.0;
    c = 18.0;
  }
  public double evaluate (double x) // method for a quadratic calculation
  { return a * x * x + b * x + c; }
  public double linear_only (double x) // method for a linear calculation
  { return b * x + c; }
} // End quadratic class body
```

Figure 35. Class Source Code with a Package Statement

7.7.1. Putting Classes into Packages

When a Java file containing a package statement is compiled, the resulting .class file is placed in the directory specified by the package statement. The package statement in the quadratic class in Figure 35 should be placed in the directory goal. The other name **first** is also a directory. The directory names in the package statement specify the exact location of the classes in the package. If these directories do not exist before the class is compiled, the compiler creates them.

When compiling a class in a package, there is an extra option (**-d**) that must be passed to the compiler that specifies where to create all the directories in the package statement. For example, a compile command to create a package for the quadratic class and store it in **c:\first\goal** is:

javac -d c:\ quadratic.java;

Review the package compile command in Java for other options.

7.7.2. Using Packages

To use a package from a class use the import statement to import the reusable class into the program and use the class. The import statement for the **quadratic class** in the **c:\first\goal** directory is

```
import first.goal.quadratic;
```

In the case, where many classes are used from the same directory use the wile card form

```
import first.goal.*;
```

Use the **quadratic class** to make a calculation in a class called **show_data**.

```
import first.goal.*;
import javax.swing.*;
public class show_data
{ public static void main (String args [ ])
  {
    double value = 0.0;
    quadratic ref = new quadratic ( );
    value = ref.evaluate (8.0);
    System.out.println ("The quadratic value calculation is " + value);
  }
}
```

Some useful Java system package names are detailed in Figure 36.

Package Name	Contents
java.applet	Classes for implementing applets
java.awt	Classes for graphics, windows, and GUIs
java.awt.event	Classes that support the AWT event-handling model
java.awt.image	Classes for image processing
java.awt.peer	Interface definitions for platform-independent GUIs
java.io	Classes for input and output
java.lang	Basic language classes (such as Math)
java.net	Classes for networking
java.util	Useful auxiliary such as Date

Abstract Windows Toolkit (AWT)
Graphics User Interface (GUI)

Figure 36. Some Java System Package Names

Java offers a way to use classes in a particular package without having to use their fully qualified names. The import statement is used for this purpose. The syntax for the import statement is

```
import package_name.*;
```

This import statement allows all the classes in the package to be used without qualifying their names. Another form of the import statement is

```
import package_name.class_name;
```

7.8. Exercises

1. Write a class application to calculate the volume and surface area of a sphere of radius **r**. Store the class in a package name **jgen**.

2. Write a class application to calculate the radius of a sphere with a known volume. Store the class in a package name **jgen**.

3. Write a class application to calculate the perimeter and area of a rectangle given a length and a width. Store the class in a package name **rgen.geom**.

4. Write a class application to calculate the area of a right triangle given two sides of the triangle. Store the class in a package name **rgen.geom**.

5. Write an application to calculate the area of a right triangle using the class application in package **rgen.geom** from problem 4. Read inputs from a non-keyboard input device. Display inputs and results.

6. Write an application to calculate the volume of a sphere using the class in package **jgen** from problem 1. Read inputs from a non-keyboard input device. Display inputs and results.

7. Write an application to calculate the radius of a sphere using the class from problem 2. Read inputs from a non-keyboard input device. Display inputs and results.

8. Write an application to calculate the volume of a sphere using the class in package **jgen** from problem 1. Read inputs from a non-keyboard input device. Display inputs and results.

9. Write an application to calculate the perimeter of a rectangle given a length and a width using the class in package **rgen.geom** from problem 3. Read inputs from a non-keyboard input device. Display inputs and results.

10. Write an application to calculate the area of a sphere and the area of a rectangle using packages **jgen** and **rgen.geom** from problems 1 and 3. Read inputs from a non-keyboard input device. Display inputs and results.

8
Arrays and String

8.1. Introduction

An array is a group of contiguous memory locations that have the same name and the same type. A location or element in an array is referred to by specifying the name and the position number or index of the element in the array. Java arrays are zero origin. The position number or index expression sometimes called a **subscript** of the first element of an array is zero. A location is specified as **name** [**index**]. The **index** is enclosed in brackets after the array **name**. The first location is **name** [0] in every array.

Figure 37 details an array **h** of ten elements. The 9th element in the array is **h** [**9**]. For example, if we assume that variable **a** is equal to 2 and the variable **b** is equal to 4, then the statement

```
h [a + b] = 9;
```

store 9 in array element 6.

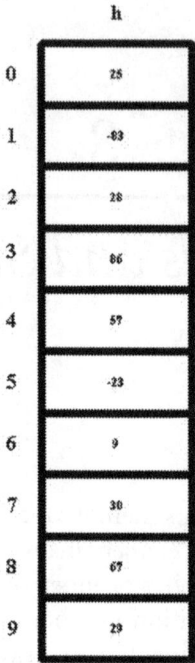

Figure 37. A 10-Element Array

The length of the array h is c.length. The value of h [3] is 86, the value of h [5] is -23, and the value of h [9] is 29. To calculate the sum of the values contained in the last 4 elements of array h and store the result in variable total, we would write

```
total = h [6] + h [7] + h [8] + h [9];
```

8.2. Declaring and Creating Arrays

To create an array, the reference to the array must be declared. The array can then be instantiated using the new operator, which allocates memory space to store values. A Java statement that declared and created the array h in Figure 37 is

```
int [ ] h = new int [10];
```

8.3. Initializing and Processing Arrays

After an array is created, values may be stored into array elements. For example, initialize **h** in Figure 37 to values that are the position number or index plus 20 with for loop.

```
for (int j = 0; j < h.length; j++)
    h [j] = j + 20;
```

Another technique for instantiating arrays is using an initializer list that provides the initial values for the elements of the array. This is similar to initializing a variable of a primitive data type in its declaration except an array requires several values.

The items in the initializer list are separated by commas and the list is delimited by braces. An initializer list can be used when an array is first declared. For example, the array **h** in Figure 37 could be initialized with:

```
int [ ] h = {25, -83, 28, 86, 57, -23, 9, 30, 67, 29};
```

The type of each value must match the type of the array. For example, declare and initialize an array **letters** with 7 characters.

```
char [ ] letters = {'D', 'F', 'H', 'A', 'M', 'P', 'T'};
```

8.4. Array of Objects

In Section 8.3, arrays of primitive type elements were created. Some implementations require array of objects. For example, create an array **quad_array** of 20 quadratic objects:

```
quadratic [ ] quad_array = new quadratic [20];
```

Initialize the quad_array with a for loop:

```
for (int m = 0; m < quad_array.length; m++)
{ quad_array [m] = new quadratic ( ); }
```

8.5. Copying Arrays

In Java, you can copy primitive data type variables using assignment statements. Objects such as arrays cannot be copied using assignment statements. Assigning one object to another object generates a pointer to the same memory location. Arrays may be copied with for loops. For example, copy the elements in an allocated array **sray** to an allocated array **tray**.

```
int [ ] sray = {4, 6, 8, 10, 12, 14, 16, 18, 20};
int [ ] tray = new int [8];
for (int k = 0; k < sray.length; k++)
    tray [k] = sray [k];
```

Java offers an efficient way to copy arrays. Use the **System.arraycopy ( )** method to copy arrays instead of using a loop. The syntax for **arraycopy ( )** is:

```
arraycopy (sourcearray, src_pos, targetarray, tar_pos, length);
```

The parameter **src_pos** is the starting position in **sourcearray** and **tar_pos** is the starting position in the **targetarray**. The parameter **length** is the number of elements copied from **sourcearray** to **targetarray**. For example, the elements of **sray** are copied to **tray** with:

```
double [ ] sray = {3.0, 6.0, 105.2, 34.6, 209.8};
double [ ] tray = new double [sray.length];
System.arraycopy (sray, 0, tray, 0, sray.length);
```

The target array must be created and memory space allocated before it is used as the target parameter in the arraycopy method.

8.6. Multidimensional Arrays

Any array with more than one dimension is called a **multidimensional array**. A two-dimensional array could be viewed as a table with rows and columns. The row position number or index is the row reference. The column position number or index is the column reference. The row and column indices are call subscripts. A two-dimensional array **m** is detailed in Figure 38.

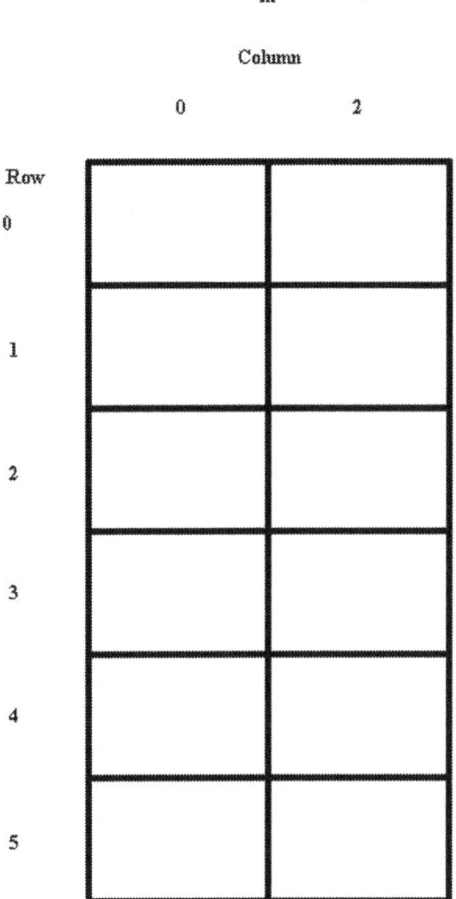

Figure 38. A Two-dimensional Array

Every element in array **m** is identified in Figure 38 by an element name of the form m [i] [j], where **m** is the array name and **i** and **j** are the subscripts that uniquely identify the row and column of each element in **m**. Notice that the names of the elements in the first row all have a first subscript of 0. With a fixed row number of 0 every element of the first row of **m** can be subscripted by varying the subscript **j**. With a fixed column number **j** of 0 every element of the first column of **m** can be subscripted by varying subscript **i**.

Multiple-subscripted arrays can be initialized in declarations. Double-subscripted array p [2] [2] could be declared and initialized with

```
int p [ ] [ ] = {{5, 9}, {6, 3}};
```

The values are grouped by row in braces.

A multiple-dimensional array with the same number of rows and columns can be allocated dynamically. For example, a 4-by-4 array **s** is allocated as follows:

```
int [ ] [ ] s = new int [4] [4];
```

Initialize the array **s** with the product of the row and column subscript with for loop.

```
for (int i = 0; i < 4; i++)
   for (int j = 0; j < 4; j++)
      s [i] [j] = i * j;
```

8.7. The String Class

The **class String** is defined as a Java package in **java.lang.String**. This package is automatically imported into every Java program that is compiled with the Java compiler. A String object is created using the keyword new and the String constructor method. For example, define an object named **speak**, declare it to be of type String, and assign an initial value of "Welcome" to the String.

```
String speak = new String ("Welcome");
```

Alternatively, you can declare a String literal containing "Welcome" with the statement

```
String speak = "Welcome";
```

Create an array of Strings. For example, store three street names as a String named **streets**.

```
String [ ] streets = {"Washington Place", "Independence Avenue",
                      "Maryland Avenue"};
```

The street names can be accessed like any other array object. For example, print the street names in **streets**.

```
for (int d = 0; d < streets.length; ++d)
    System.out.println (streets [d]);
```

8.7.1. String Comparisons

String is a class, and each created String is a class object. A **String variable** refers to a location in memory rather than a particular value. The content of two String cannot be compared with comparison operators. Compare **string_in** to **string_out** for equality.

```
if (string_in == string_out)
   System.out.println ("string_in and string_out are the same object")
else
   System.out.println ("string_in and string_out are not equal");
```

The == operator checks whether **string_in** and **string_out** refer to the same object. This operator does not indicate whether **string_in** and **string_out** contain the same content when they are different objects. Use the **equals ( )** method for the comparison of the contents of objects.

```
if (string_in.equals (string_out))
   System.out.println ("string_in and string_out have the same content")
else
   System.out.println ("string_in and string_out are not equal");
```

The **compareTo ( )** method can be used to compare methods.

```
int g = string_in.compareTo (string_out);
```

The variable **g** is assigned 0 if **string_in** is equal to **string_out**. When **g** is less than zero **string_in** is lexicographically less than **string_out**, and **g** is greater than zero implies that **string_in** is lexicographically greater than **string_out**. The Java string class offers other methods for comparing string.

8.7.2. String Concatenation

A character string, delimited by the double quotation character, cannot be split between two lines of code. This problem can be solved with the string concatenation operator, the plus sign (+). String concatenation produces one string in which the second string is appended to the first. An example of string concatenation is detailed in the **println ( )** method as:

```
int x = 12;
int y = 30;
System.out.println ("This is a string " + x+y + " concatenation
                    example ");
```

Primitive type data such as **int, double,** and **float** are not Strings. At times, you want to convert primitive type data to strings. For example, convert **int** data to a **String**.

```
int key = 45;
String strkey = toString (key);
```

8.7.3. Substrings

The substring method creates a new String object by copying part of an existing String object. The default argument is based on the fact that a String's first position is position zero. For example, print the first five letters and letters ten through twelve of the street names in **streets**.

```
String [ ] streets = {"Washington Place", "Independence Avenue",
                      "Maryland Avenue"};
String extract;
for (int d = 0; d < streets.length; ++d)
{ extract = streets[d].substring (4); // first five characters
  System.out.println (extract);
  extract = streets[d].substring (10, 12); // characters 10 through 12
  System.out.println (extract);
}
```

8.7.4. String Length and Retrieving Individual Characters in a String

Define a String letters = "Java Strings"; The length of **letters** is letters.length ( ), the number of characters in **letters**. To retrieve a specific character in a string **letters** use the letters.charAt (index) method, where **index** is the location of the character in **letters**. The range of **index** is between 0 and letters.length ( ) - 1.

8.8. The StringBuffer Class

In the String class, the value of a String is fixed after the String is created. Create a String notice = "Welcome"; with the goal of creating "Welcome to Java". To accomplish this goal the first String referenced by **notice** must be modified. Create a Sting notice = "to Java";, you have not changed the contents of the memory location at **notice**, nor have you eliminated the characters "Welcome". The characters "to Java" are stored at a different memory location and the new address is in the **notice** variable. To create "Welcome to Java" a new String notice = "Welcome to Java" must be created.

The **StringBuffer class** offers an alternative to the String class that avoids fixed Strings. StringBuffer is flexible because it allows you to append new contents into a **StringBuffer**. The **StringBuffer class** provides overload methods to append many types. For example, a code segment that appends strings and characters into **mybuf** to form a new string, "Welcome to Java" is:

```
StringBuffer mybuf = new StringBuffer ( );
mybuf.append ("Welcome");
mybuf.append (' ');
mybuf.append ("to");
mybuf.append (' ');
mybuf.append ("Java");
```

Every string buffer has a capacity. The buffer is automatically increased to accommodate additional characters. **StringBuffer** provides many methods for manipulating string buffers. For example, **capacity ( )**, **reverse ( )**, **length ( )**, **charAt ( )**, **insert ( )**, and other methods.

8.9. The StringTokenizer Class

The **StringTokenizer class** is a part of the **java.util** package. This package must be available at the beginning of the program. Provide the **java.util** package with:

```
import java.util;
```

This class is used to divide a line of text into words or tokens. In some cases a token is a series of characters separated from its neighbors by a delimiter such as white space or blank, end of lines, or tabs. For example, a string of text is initialized with words separated by a space. Print the tokens in the string **text_in**.

```
String text_in = "Welcome to Java and Complete Objects";
StringTokenizer small_unit = new StringTokenizer (text_in);
System.out.println ("The number of tokens is " +
            small_unit.countTokens ( ));
```

```
System.out.println ("The tokens are: ");
while (small_unit.hasMoreTokens ( ))
{
   System.out.println (small_unit.nextToken ( ));
}
```

8.10. Command-Line Arguments

The Java **main** ( ) method is declared with an array of Strings as its arguments.

```
public static void main (String [ ] args) { }
```

The **main** ( ) method has parameters like a regular method. Actual parameters may be passed to a **main** ( ) method.

8.10.1. Passing Arguments to Java Programs

Parameters may be passed to a Java program from the command line when you run the program. For example, the Java compiled and build program name is **react** that executes with two arguments **arg0** and **arg1** from the command line.

```
java react arg0 arg1
```

The arguments **arg0** and **arg1** are strings. These strings may not be in double quotes on the command line. The arguments are separated by a space. If the argument itself contains a space, you must use double quotes to group all items in the argument. For example, the input to **react** is argument **first program** and **software**.

```
java react "first program" software
```

8.10.2. Processing Command-Line Parameters

Arguments are passed to the **main** ( ) method are stored in an array of **Strings args**. The order of the argument is the array index of the string. The first argument is **arg [0]**, and the number of arguments passed is **args.length**. The programmer must retrieve the parameters from the array of Strings and use it to accomplish program goals.

8.11. Exercises

All application components are implemented using methods. Data used in several applications are generated with a uniform random number generator. For example, to generate uniform random numbers between one and five use:

int e = 1 + int (Math.random ( ) * 5);

1. Write a program that initializes an array with 50 integers. Use a uniform random number generator to generate the integers of 1 to 3 digits. Display the numbers in descending order.

2. Write a program that implements the requirements:
   1. Create a class for students. The class must contain the student's **name** (String), and **ID** (int), **street** (String), **city** (String), and **State** (String).
   2. Create 10 students **name, ID, street, city,** and **State**. The ID is a unique uniform random number with one to three digits.
   3. Arrange the students in ascending order of IDs.
   4. Display the **name, ID,** and **State** for each student.

3. Write a program that implements the requirements:
   1. Write code to multiple two int square matrices. The method is declared as:

      ```
      public static matrix multiply (matrix h1, matrix h2)
      ```

      The algorithm for matrix multiplication can be described as:

      ```
      for (int i - 0; i < h.length; i++)
         for (int j = 0; j < h.length; j++)
         { p [i, j] = 0;
            for (int k = 0; k < h.length; k++)
               p [i, j] = p [i, j] + h1 [i, k] * h2 [k, j];
         }
      ```

   2. Write a main method in the same class to initialize the matrices using a uniform random number generator with one to two digit numbers, calculate and produce the product matrix, and display the product matrix.

4. Write a program to implement requirements as:
   1. Calculate the product of the diagonal elements of a square matrix. A method may be declared as:

      ```
      public static int dialcal (matrix h1)
      ```

      An algorithm for to calculate the sum of the product of the diagonal elements of a square matrix is:

      ```
      int dproduct = 0;
      for (int i = 0; i < h.length; i++)
         dproduct = dproduct + h1 [i, i] * h1 [i, i];
      ```

   2. Write a main method in the same class to initialize the matrix using a uniform random number generator to number with one to three digits, calculate the sum of the diagonal elements of the matrix, and display the matrix and the sum of the product of the diagonal elements.

5. Write an application that meets the requirements as:
   1. Calculate the average of 20 int numbers in an array.
   2. Write a main method in the same class that initializes the array with integers, calculate the average of the number in the array, and display the numbers and the average.

6. Write a program that implements requirements as:
   1. Calculate the average of 20 int numbers in an array y1.
   2. Write a method to initialize the array y1 with integers.
   3. Calculate the difference of the array y1 and the average of the elements in array y1. Store the difference in an array d1.
   4. Write a main method in the same class to invoke your methods, display arrays y1, d1 and the average of the elements in y1.

7. Write a program that reads 100 integers into an array. Display the numbers in the array and any duplicates.

8. A car dealership has a car collection. Write an application using methods to initialize an array with numbers that represent the cars horsepower. Calculate the average horsepower and display the average and the horsepower of all cars.

9. Design and implement an application that reads numbers in the range one to 50. Count how many occurrences of each number were read. After all numbers have been processed, display all of the numbers that were generated and the number of times each unique number was read.

10. Design and implement an application that computes and displays the mean and standard deviation of at least 50 integers stored in an array x. The numbers are read into x. Compute both mean and standard deviation as floating point values using the formulas:

$$\text{mean} = (1/n) \sum_{n-1}^{n} x_i$$

$$\text{sd} = \left(\sum_{i=1}^{n}(x_i - \text{mean})^2 / (n-1)\right)^{\frac{1}{2}}$$

11. Tall Bank can handle up to 30 customers who have savings accounts. The bank holds a record for each customer. The information maintained in the bank is customer **ID** (int), **name** (String), **street** (String), **State** (String), and **savings** (double). Design and implement methods to deposit into and withdraw from the savings account for withdraw from the savings account for each user. Produce the appropriate error messages for invalid transactions.

12. Design and implement an application using methods to create an array that stores 20 prices. Read the prices from an input device. All prices are dollars end cents between one dollar and 10 dollars. Display all values less than five dollars. Calculate the average of the prices, and display all values higher than the calculated average value.

13. Write a program using methods that lets the user enter numbers one through nine, one at a time, and then display the numbers that the user entered. Store the numbers in an array. Write the appropriate error messages for more than 10 numbers and invalid numbers.

14. Write a **toString ( )** method that creates a string representation of a matrix. Each row should end with a \n character.

15. Write a program to read data items in two arrays **t** and **s**. Store the product of corresponding elements of **t** and **s** in a third array **u**. Display a three column table that details the corresponding elements of the arrays **t**, **s**, and **u**. Compute and display the square root of the sum of the items in **u**.

16. Write a program that takes 10 integers as input. The program places the even integers into an array called **aeven**, the odd integers into an array called **aodd**, and the negative integers into an array called **anegat**. The program displays the contents of the three arrays after all of the integers have been entered. Display the count of the number of items in the **aeven**, **aodd**, and **anegat** arrays.

9

Class Inheritance

9.1. Introduction

Inheritance is a form of software reusability in which new classes are created with attributes and behaviors from existing classes. Software reusability saves time, produces high-quality products, and reduces maintenance problems. **Polymorphism** enables us to write programs in a general way to handle a wide variety of existing and specified related classes. This makes it easy to add new capabilities to existing systems.

New classes may be created without writing new instance variables and methods. The programmer can use a Java programming language keyword with a class name in the head of the class definition in the new classes to inherit the instance variables and instance methods from a previously defined base class or superclass. The new class created with the Java keyword followed by the superclass name is called a **derived class** or subclass. Each subclass is a candidate to be a superclass for another subclass. This creates a class hierarchy.

The **direct superclass** of a subclass is the class named with the Java keyword called **extends** in which the instance variables and methods are inherited. An indirect subclass is inherited from two or more levels up the class hierarchy. For example, define a **class E** as a subclass of a **class H**.

```
class E extends H
{ // E is a subclass of H
   ...
}
```

The body of E follows the usual syntax. The new part is **extends H** in the class header. Class E is a subclass of H, the objects of E contain all the instance variables of objects of H as well as the instance variables declared in E, and the objects respond to all instance methods defined in H as well as those defined in E.

9.2. Superclasses and Subclasses

Programmers can reuse or change the methods of superclasses, add new data and new methods in the subclasses. For example, create a linear subclass of the base class quadratic created in Figure 34.

```
public class linear extends quadratic
{ private double control;
  // default constructor
  public linear ( )
  { super ( );
    control = 0.0;
  }

  // constructor
  public linear (double quad)
  { super (quad);
    control = 1.0;
  }

  // calculate linear
  public double linall ( )
  { return linear_only (quad) * control; }
}
```

The Java keyword extends tells the compiler that the linear class is derived from the quadratic class and inherits data and methods from quadratic. A subclass is not a subset of its superclass. The keyword super refers to the superclass of the class in which super appears. The keyword **super** can be used to call a superclass constructor or a superclass method.

9.3. Calling Superclass Constructors

The syntax to call a superclass constructor is:

```
super (parameters);
```

In Section 9.2, **super ( )** and **super (quad)** are used to call the constructors from the quadratic class to initialize the parameter of the quadratic class to make it linear. The call **super ( )** must appear in the first line of the constructor. This is the only way to invoke a superclass's constructor.

9.3.1. Calling Superclass Methods

The keyword supper can be used to reference a non-constructor method in the superclass. The syntax is:

```
super.method (parameters);
```

Rewrite the linall method in the linear class as:

```
public double linall ( )
{ return super.linear_only (quad) * control; }
```

It is not necessary to insert super before linear_only (quad), because it is a method in the quadratic class and can be accessed in the linear class.

Superclasses are referenced with the keyword **super**. The current class is referenced with the keyword **this**. For example, the constructor can be redefined in the quadratic class as:

```
quadratic ( )                    // constructor
{ a = 1.0;
  b = 5.0;
  c = 6.0;
  this (1.0);
}
quadratic (double myvalue)       // constructor
{ a = myvalue;
  b = 9.0;
  c = 18.0;
  this.myvalue = myvalue;
}
```

9.4. The Object class

In Java, all classes are derived from the **Object class**. Any class definition that doesn't use the **extends** keyword to derive itself explicitly from another class, the class is automatically derived from the Object class by default. For example, define two equivalent classes.

```
class light
{ // class body
}

class light extends Object
{ // class body
}
```

Any public method of Object can be invoked through any object created in any Java program. The **Object class** is defined in the **java.lang** package of the Java standard class library. Some methods of the Object class are:

```
boolean equals (Object obj)
```
Returns true if this object is an alias of the specified object.

```
String toString ( )
```
Returns a string representation of this object.

```
Object clone ( )
```
Creates and returns a copy of this object.

9.5. The final and abstract Modifiers

Two modifiers used with respect to class inheritance are final and abstract.

The final modifier may be used in declaring constants. Class inheritance may be controlled. The final modifier of a class indicates that the class cannot be a parent class or it cannot be extended.

An abstract modifier of a class is used to allow extends and prevents the creation of a class instance. An **abstract class** is one from which you cannot create any concrete objects, but from which you can inherit. Non-abstract classes from which objects can be instantiated are called **concrete classes**. If you provide an empty method within an abstract class, the method is an abstract method even if you do not explicitly use the keyword abstract when defining the method. For example, see Figure 24.

9.6. Casting Objects

You have used the casting operator to convert variables of one primitive type to another primitive type. Objects may be cast to convert an object of one class type to another within an inheritance hierarchy. The syntax is similar to the one used for casting among primitive data types. Enclose the target object type in parentheses and place it before the object to be cast. For example:

```
linear my_linear = (quadratic) my_quad;
```

This statement converts my_quad to its superclass variable my_linear. For the casting to work, you must make sure that the object to be cast is an instance of the subclass.

9.7. Processing Numeric Values as Objects

Some Java methods require using objects as arguments. Java offers a way to wrap a primitive data type into an object. The primitive types wrap int to Integer, double to Double, boolean to Boolean, and others. For example, convert the number 85 to an object name **trans**.

```
Integer trans = new Integer (85);
```

9.8. The Numeric Class

Numeric wrapper classes common methods are generalized in an abstract superclass called number. This class defines abstract methods to convert the represented numeric value to byte, double, float, int, long, and short. These methods are implemented in the subclasses of Number. For example, byte is:

```
public byte byteValue ( )
```

This returns the value of the specified number as a byte.

9.8.1. Numeric Wrapper Class Constructors

A numeric wrapper object may be constructed from a primitive data type value or from a string representing the numeric value. The constructors are:

```
public Integer (int value);
public Integer (String z);
public Double (double value);
public Double (String z);
```

For example:

```
Integer i_obj = new Integer (65);
```

or

```
Integer i_obj = new Integer ("65");
```

9.8.2. Numeric Class Constants

Each numeric wrapper class has constants such as MIN_VALUE and MAX_VALUE representing the minimum and maximum values in the range corresponding to their primitive data type.

9.8.3. Conversion Methods

The numeric wrapper class implements the abstract methods **doubleValue ( )**, **floatValue ( )**, **intValue ( )**, **longValue ( )**, and **shortValue ( )** defined in the **Number class**. It overrides the **toString ( )** method defined in the **Object class**.

For example:

```
int ivalue = integerObject.intValue ( );
```

This assigns the int value of integerObject to i_value.

9.8.4. The valueOf ( ) and parseInt ( ) Methods

The numeric wrapper classes have a class method valueOf (String z). This method creates a new object, initialized to the value of the string. For example:

```
Double d_obj = Double.valueOf ("16.98");
```

The Integer wrapper class has some methods that are not available in Double. The method **parseInt** ( ) is available only in the Integer wrapper class. For example:

```
static int parseInt (String z, int radix);
```

The method **parseInt** ( ) returns the integer value represented by the string z in the specified radix. If the radix is omitted, base 10 is the default.

9.9. Exercises

1. Write an application that inherits from the right triangle class in package rgen.geom from Chapter 7 on Object-Oriented Programming and problem 4 to calculate the third side of a right triangle. Read inputs from a non-keyboard input device. Display inputs and results.

2. Write an application that inherits from the sphere class in package jgen from Chapter 7 on Object-Oriented Programming and problem 1 to calculate the volume and surface area of a sphere. Read inputs from a non-keyboard input device. Display inputs and results.

3. Write an application that inherits from the sphere class in package jgen from Chapter 7 on Object-Oriented Programming and problems 1 and 2 to calculate the radius and surface area of a sphere. Read inputs from a non-keyboard input device. Display inputs and results.

4. Write an application that inherits from the sphere class in package jgen from Chapter 7 on Object-Oriented Programming and problems 1 to calculate the volume of a sphere. Read inputs from a non-keyboard input device. Display inputs and results.

5. Write an application that inherits from the rectangle class in package rgen.geom from Chapter 7 on Object-Oriented Programming and problems 3 to calculate the perimeter of a rectangle given a length and a width. Read inputs from a non-keyboard input device. Display inputs and results.

6. Write an application that inherits from the sphere and rectangle classes in packages jgen and rgen.geom from Chapter 7 on Object-Oriented Programming and problems 1 and 3 to calculate the surface area of a sphere and the area of a rectangle. Read inputs from a non-keyboard input device. Display inputs and results.

10

Basic Graphical User Interface Components

10.1. Introduction

A **Java applet** is a Java program that is intended to be embedded into a Hypertext Markup Language (HTML) document. The HTML is transported across a network and executed using an **appletviewer** or **Web browser**. An applet and Java application program are different. A Java application program is a stand-alone program that can be executed using the Java interpreter.

The Java **Abstract Windowing Toolkit (AWT)** package contains the classes and interfaces required to create and manipulate graphical user interfaces in earlier versions of Java. The classes in AWT can still be used, but the **Swing GUI** components of the **javax.swing** packages are often used instead.

The Java Swing GUI Components package contains classes and interfaces for Java's Swing GUI components that provide support for portable GUIs. Some basic GUI components are detailed in Figure 39.

Component	Description
JLabel	An area where uneditable text of icons can be displayed.
JTextField	An area in which data are displayed or the user inputs data from the keyboard.
JButton	An area that triggers an event when clicked.
JCheckBox	A GUI component that is either selected or not selected.
JComboBox	A drop-down list of items from which the user can make a selection.
JList	An area where a list of items is displayed from which the user can make a selection.
JPanel	A container to which components can be placed.

Figure 39. Some Basic GUI Components

10.2. The Applet Class

Applets are classes that inherit from the **class JApplet**. The **class JApplet** is located in the **javax.swing.JApplet** package. The package is imported with the import statement.

```
import javax.swing.JApplet;
```

In most cases, JApplet class methods **init**, **start**, **paint**, **stop**, and **destroy** are overwritten by new versions of the methods in the new subclass applet. An Applet life cycle is detailed in Figure 40.

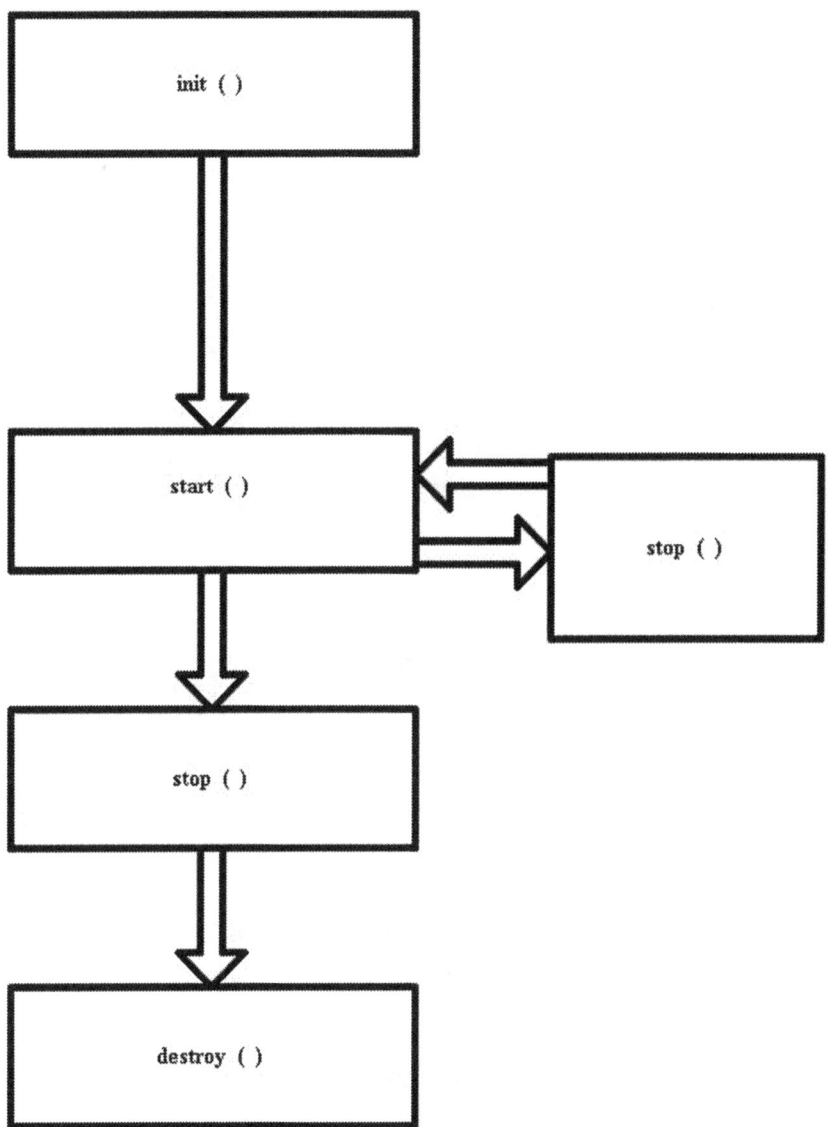

Figure 40. Applet Life Cycle

10.2.1. The init ( ) Method

The init ( ) method acts like a class constructor to initialize values of inheritance variables. This method is invoked automatically when the applet is run.

10.2.2. The start ( ) Method

The start ( ) method initializes features used in concurrent executions or animations.

10.2.3. The paint ( ) Method

This method is called once, after init ( ) completes. The paint ( ) method is called each time the repaint ( ) method is called. Output of test or drawings is created in the paint ( ) method with an object instantiated from the Graphics class.

10.2.4. The stop ( ) Method

The stop ( ) method is called to terminate the applet execution.

10.2.5. The destroy ( ) Method

The destroy ( ) method reclaims the resources after the applet is removed from memory.

10.2.6. Example Applet and <applet> HTML Tag

An applet class named **first_apple** that overrides the **init** ( ) method and the **paint** ( ) is detailed in Figure 41.

Implementation steps for a Java applet called first_apple are:

1. Define the head of a Java applet class called **first_apple** including Java import packages and inheritance.

   ```
   import javax.swing.*;
   import java.awt.*;

   public class first_apple extends JApplet
   {
   ```

2. Define the applet **init** ( ) method with a void Java method type modifier.
   ```
   public void init ( )
   {
     // Body of the initialization method
   } // End init method
   ```

3. Define the applet paint method with a void Java method type modifier.
   ```
   public void paint (Graphics gc)
   {
     // Body of the drawing method
   } // End paint method
   ```

4. Define the tail for the Java applet class.

   }

A detail program for the Java applet class saved with a file name first_apple.java.

```
// first_apple class
import javax.swing.*;
import java,awt.*;

public class first_apple extends JApplet
{
  // Instance variables

  public void init ( )
  {
    // Body of the initialization method
  } // End init method

  public void paint (Graphics gc)
  {
    // Body of the drawing method
  } // End paint method

}
```

Figure 41. Example Applet

Applets are embedded in HTML and executed in an appletviewer or browser. HTML documents are saved in files with name followed by an extension .html or **.htm**. A HTML program has a header, body, and a tail statement. Many statements in HTML are of the form

```
<statement name and attributes> statement context information
</statement name>
```

The applet HTML tag is:

```
<applet code = "class name" width = 460 height = 200> </applet>
```

Class name is the compiled class name, width is the horizontal length of the applet window, and height is the vertical length of the applet window.

For example, a HTML program that embeds **first_apple** is:

```
<html>
<body>
<applet code = "first_apple.class" width = 460 height = 200>
</applet>
</body>
</html>
```

10.2.7. Applets with User Input and Output with GUI

Consider an example of an age conversion applet that receives the user's age in years as input and outputs the age in months. Dialog boxes are used to interact with the user of the applet. Dialog boxes are windows that typically are used to display important messages to the user of an application. Class **JOptionPane** allows you to easily display a dialog box containing information. Class JOptionPane is defined in a package called **javax.swing**. A user labeled JTexfield is posted in a browser window to receive the user's age. Standard applet methods **init ( )** and **actionPerformed** a user defined method **convert ( )** performs the calculation. The age of the user is entered into a Graphics User Interface (GUI) box in the applet. This box is a component of the **JTextfield class** and the label is a component of the Label class. The detail program is a class called **age_cal**. The class age_cal is implemented with classes from the **java.applet** package

Implementation steps for a Java applet class called **age_cal** to calculate a user's age in months from an age in years.

1. Define the head of a Java applet class called **age_cal** including Java import packages and inheritance. Implement an ActionListener to define event processing for Buttons.

   ```
   import java.applet.*;
   import javax.swing.*;
   import java.awt.*;
   import java.awt.event.*;
   // Class to input age in years.
   public class age_cal extends Applet
     implements ActionListener
   {
     Label note;             // Declare user prompt.
     TextField intext;       // Declare input box.
     int age;                // Declare the age input variable.
   ```

2. Allocate a Button with an initial OK.

   ```
   private Button press = new Button ("OK");
   ```

3. Define the applet **init ( )** method with a void Java method type modifier.

   ```
   public void init ( )
   {
   ```

4. Allocate a Label called **note**.

   ```
   note = new Label ("Enter age in years and press Enter");
   ```

5. Allocate a TextField called **intext**.

   ```
   intext = new TextField (6);
   ```

6. Place the label, text field and button on the applet. Post a form with a label, text field and a button.

   ```
   add (note);
   add (intext);
   add (press);
   ```

7. Define an ActionListener handler for the button.

   ```
   press.addActionListener (this);
   ```

8. Define the tail of the init method.

    ```
    } // End of init method
    ```

9. Define the head of an actionPerformed method to process events.

    ```
    public void actionPerformed (ActionEvent e)
    {
    ```

10. Get the year information from the text area.

    ```
    String years = intext.getText ( );
    ```

11. Display the number of years in a dialog box.

    ```
    JOptionPane.showMessageDialog(null, "Number of years: " + years);
    ```

12. Get the information from the TextField.

    ```
    age = Integer.parseInt (intext.getText ( ));
    ```

13. Convert the years to months by calling the convert method.

    ```
    String months = convert (age);
    ```

14. Display months in a dialog box.

    ```
    JOptionPane.showMessageDialog(null, "Number of months: " + months);
    ```

15. Display the number of months in a status bar.

    ```
    showStatus ("Number of Months: " + convert (age)); // Months
    intext.setText (" "); // Clear entry box.
    ```

16. Define the tail of the actionPeformed method.

    ```
    } // End action method
    ```

17. Define a method head to convert age in years to months with declarations.

    ```
    public String convert (int age)
    {
       int vert;
    ```

18. Convert the age in years to months.

    ```
    vert = age * 12;
    ```

19. Create an object for the number of months.

    ```
    Integer ver = new Integer (vert);
    ```

20. Create a string from the object using toString ( ).

    ```
    String conv = ver.toString ( );
    ```

21. Return a string for the number of months.

    ```
    return conv;
    ```

22. Define a tail for the convert method.

    ```
    } // End convert method
    ```

23. Define the tail for the age_cal applet class.

    ```
    } // End age_cal class
    ```

A Java applet classis detailed to calculate a user's age in months from an age in years. This Java applet is stored in a file name **age_cal.java**.

```
// The age_cal class
import java.applet.*;
import javax.swing.*;
import java.awt.*;
import java.awt.event.*;
// Class to input age in years.
public class age_cal extends Applet
   implements ActionListener
{
  Label note;              // Declare user prompt.
  TextField intext;        // Declare input box.
  int age;                 // Declare the age input variable.
  private Button press = new Button ("OK");
  // Set up GUI components in the init ( ) method.
  public void init ( )
   {
     note = new Label ("Enter age in years and press Enter");
     intext = new TextField (6);
```

```
    // Place the label and text field on the applet.
    add (note);
    add (intext);
    add (press);

    press.addActionListener (this);
} // End of init method

// Action to user input.
public void actionPerformed (ActionEvent e)
{ // Get the year information from the text area.
    String years = intext.getText( );
    // Display the number of years in a dialog box.
    JOptionPane.showMessageDialog(null, "Number of years: " + years);

    // Get the information from the TextField.
    age = Integer.parseInt (intext.getText ( ));
    // Convert the years to months.
    String months = convert (age);
    // Display months in a dialog box.
    JOptionPane.showMessageDialog(null, "Number of months: " + months);
    // Display the number of months in a status bar.
    showStatus ("Number of Months: " + convert (age)); // Months
    intext.setText (" ");// Clear entry box.
} // End actionPerformed method

// Method to convert age in years to months.
public String convert (int age)
{
    int vert;
    vert = age * 12;
    Integer ver = new Integer (vert);
    String conv = ver.toString ( );
    return conv;
} // End convert method
} // End age_cal class
```

Label from the **Label class** indicates what is to be entered into the input box. **Textfield** from the **Textfield class** holds the input to the **init ( )** method.

Jabel identifier is **note** and the Jextfield identifier is **intext**.

In the **init ( )** method **note** Label is instantiated with a string constant and **intext** Textfield is instantiated with up to 6 characters. The label and text field are not placed on the screen until the **add** lines are executed. The **actionPerformed** method has one parameters **ActionEvent e.** Text is retrieved from the TextField with **getText ( )**. This **actionPerformed** method is void with no return.

A screen views of the age_cal class execution with input 55 is:

Input the age 55 years.

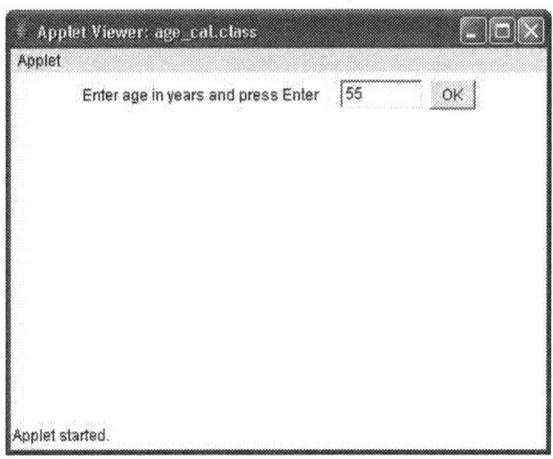

Click OK on the window and display the age input in years in a dialog box.

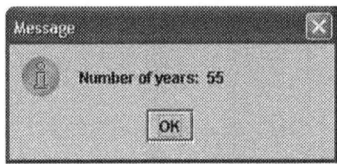

Click OK on the dislog box and convert the input age in years to months and display the result.

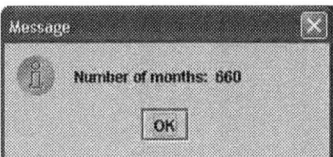

Click OK on the dialog box and display the age in months in the status bar of the age_cal window.

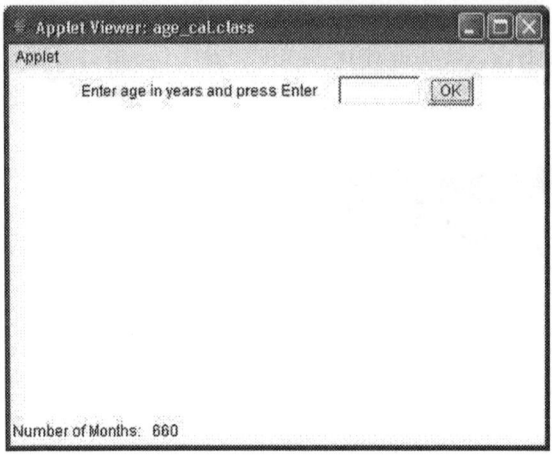

10.2.8. Running a Program as an Applet

Compile the applet as a class.

```
javac age_cal.java
```

Insert the compile class name in the HTML program.

```
<html>
<body>
<applet code = "age_cal.class" width = 460 height = 200> </applet>
</body>
</html>
```

Save the HTML program with a file name and an extension of **.html** or **htm**. Access the HTML file from the appletviewer or browser and interact with the applet dialog.

10.3. Swing Overview

This section explains the concepts you need to use Swing components in building a user interface. We use Swing components in simple programs to create user interfaces using components in the javax.swing package. Several

Swing components, such as buttons, labels, and text areas are covered. The handling of events is also discussed, as are layout management and accessibility. Some basic Swing GUI components are detailed in Figure 39.

Common superclasses of many of the Swing components are java.awt.Component extends java.lang.Object; java.awt.Container estends java.awt.Component; and javax.swing.JComponent extends java.awt.Container.

Two methods in class Component are paint and repaint. These are common operations in most GUI components. A **Container** is a collection of related components. Applications are placed in a Container by attaching components to the content pane. A method add in the Container class is used to attach a component to a content pane.

The **class JComponent** is the superclass to most Swing components. Subclass JComponents supports a pluggable look and feel that can be used to customize the look and feel when the program executes on different platforms.

Java Foundation Classes (JFC), which encompasses a group of features for building graphical user interfaces, adds rich graphics functionality and interactivity to Java applications.

Java 2D application program interface (API) enables developers to easily incorporate high-quality 2D graphics, text, and images in applications and applets. Java 2D includes extensive APIs for generating and sending high-quality output to printing devices.

Drag-and-drop support provides the ability to drag and drop between Java applications and native applications.

10.4. JOptionPane

Class JOptionPane is stored in the **javax.swing** package. JOptionPane makes it easy to pop up a standard dialog box that prompts users for a value or informs them of something.

The JOptionPane class has large number of methods; almost all uses of this class are one-line calls to one of the static showXxxDialog methods detailed in Figure 42.

Method Name	Description
showConfirmDialog	Asks a confirming question, like yes/no/cancel.
showInputDialog	Prompt for some input.
showMessageDialog	Tell the user about something that has happened.
showOptionDialog	The Grand Unification of the above three.

Figure 42. Static showXxxDialog Methods

Each of these methods also comes in a showInternalXXX flavor, which uses an internal frame to hold the dialog box detailed in JInternalFrame. All dialogs are modal. Each showXxxDialog method blocks the current thread until the user's interaction is complete.

The basic appearance of these dialog boxes uses various look-and-feels. In particular, the look-and-feels will adjust the layout to accommodate the option pane's ComponentOrientation property. The parameters of the methods aid in controlling the look-and-feel.

Parameters:

The parameters to these methods follow consistent patterns:

parentComponent

The parentComponent defines the Component that is to be the parent of this dialog box. It is used in two ways: the Frame that contains it is used as the Frame parent for the dialog box, and its screen coordinates are used in the placement of the dialog box. In general, the dialog box is placed just below the component. This parameter may be null, in which case a default Frame is used as the parent, and the dialog will be centered on the screen as a descriptive message to be placed in the dialog box. In the most common usage, message is just a String or String constant. However, the type of this parameter is actually Object. Its interpretation depends on its type:

Object[ ]

An array of objects is interpreted as a series of messages one per object arranged in a vertical stack. The interpretation is recursive and each object in the array is interpreted according to its type.

Type	Meaning
Component	The Component is displayed in the dialog.
Icon	The Icon is wrapped in a JLabel and displayed in the dialog.
Others	The object is converted to a String by calling its toString method. The result is wrapped in a JLabel and displayed.
messageType	Defines the style of the message. The Look and Feel manager may lay out the dialog differently depending on this value, and will often provide a default icon. The possible values are: ERROR_MESSAGE INFORMATION_MESSAGE WARNING_MESSAGE QUESTION_MESSAGE PLAIN_MESSAGE
optionType	Defines the set of option buttons that appear at the bottom of the dialog box: DEFAULT_OPTION YES_NO_OPTION YES_NO_CANCEL_OPTION OK_CANCEL_OPTION You aren't limited to this set of option buttons. You can provide any buttons you want using the options parameter.

options	A more detailed description of the set of option buttons that will appear at the bottom of the dialog box. The usual value for the options parameter is an array of Strings. But the parameter type is an array of Objects. A button is created for each object depending on its type:
	
	Component
	    The component is added to the button row directly.
	icon
	    A JButton is created with this as its label.
	other
	    The Object is converted to a string using its toString method and the result is used to label a JButton.
	icon
	    A decorative icon to be placed in the dialog box. A default value for this is determined by the messageType parameter.

title
: The title for the dialog box.

initialValue
: The default selection (input value).

When the selection is changed, setValue is invoked, which generates a PropertyChangeEvent.

If a JOptionPane has configured to all input setWantsInput the bound property JOptionPane.INPUT_VALUE_PROPERTY can also be listened to, to determine when the user has input or selected a value.

When one of the showXxxDialog methods returns an integer, the possible values are:

```
YES_OPTION
NO_OPTION
CANCEL_OPTION
OK_OPTION
CLOSED_OPTION
```

Examples:

Show an error dialog that displays the message, 'alert':

```
JOptionPane.showMessageDialog (null, "alert", "alert",
JOptionPane.ERROR_MESSAGE);
```

Show an internal information dialog with the message, 'information':

```
JOptionPane.showInternalMessageDialog (frame, "information",
"information", JOptionPane.INFORMATION_MESSAGE);
```

Show an information panel with the options yes/no and message 'choose one':

```
JOptionPane.showConfirmDialog (null, "choose one", "choose one",
JOptionPane.YES_NO_OPTION);
```

Show an internal information dialog with the options yes/no/cancel and message 'please choose one' and title information:

```
JOptionPane.showInternalConfirmDialog (frame, "please choose one",
"information", JOptionPane.YES_NO_CANCEL_OPTION,
JOptionPane.INFORMATION_MESSAGE);
```

Show a warning dialog with the options OK, CANCEL, title 'Warning', and message 'Click OK to continue':

```
Object[ ] options = {"OK", "CANCEL"};
JOptionPane.showOptionDialog (null, "Click OK to continue",
"Warning", JOptionPane.DEFAULT_OPTION, JOptionPane.WARNING_MESSAGE,
null, options, options[0]);
```

Show a dialog asking the user to type in a String:

```
String inputValue = JOptionPane.showInputDialog ("Please input a
value");
```

Show a dialog asking the user to select a String:

```
Object[ ] possibleValues = {"First", "Second", "Third"};
Object selectedValue = JOptionPane.showInputDialog (null, "Choose
one", "Input", JOptionPane.INFORMATION_MESSAGE, null,
possibleValues, possibleValues[0]);
```

Direct Use:

To create and use an JOptionPane directly, the standard pattern is roughly as follows:

```
JOptionPane pane = new JOptionPane (arguments);
pane.set.Xxxx(…); // Configure
JDialog dialog = pane.createDialog (parentComponent, title);
dialog.show ( );
Object selectedValue = pane.getValue ( );
if(selectedValue == null)
  return CLOSED_OPTION;
// If there is not an array of option buttons:
if (options == null) {
  if (selectedValue instanceof Integer)
    return ((Integer)selectedValue).intValue ( );
  return CLOSED_OPTION;
}
// If there is an array of option buttons:
for (int counter = 0, maxCounter = options.length;
  counter < maxCounter; counter++) {
  if (options[counter].equals (selectedValue))
  return counter;
}
return CLOSED_OPTION;
```

Field Summary

Field Type	Feild
static int	**CANCEL_OPTION** Return value from class method if CANCEL is chosen.
static int	**CLOSED_OPTION** Return value from class method if user closes window without selecting anything, more than likely this should be treated as either a CANCEL_OPTION or NO_OPTION.
static int	**DEFAULT_OPTION** Type used for showConfirmDialog.
static int	**ERROR_MESSAGE** Used for error messages.
protected Icon	**icon** Icon used in pane.
static String	**ICON_PROPERTY** Bound property name for icon.
static int	**INFORMATION_MESSAGE** Used for information messages.
static String	**INITIAL_SELECTION_VALUE_PROPERTY** Bound property name for initialSelectionValue.
static String	**INITIAL_VALUE_PROPERTY** Bound property name for initialValue.
protected Object	**initialSelectionValue** Initial value to select in selectionValues.
protected Object	**initialValue** Value that should be initially selected in options.
static String	**INPUT_VALUE_PROPERTY** Bound property name for inputValue.
protected Object	**inputValue** Value the user has input.
protected Object	**message** Message to display.

static String	MESSAGE_PROPERTY	
	Bound property name for message.	
static String	MESSAGE_TYPE_PROPERTY	
	Bound property name for type.	
protected int	messageType	
	Message type.	
static int	NO_OPTION	
	Return value from class method if NO is chosen.	
static int	OK_CANCEL_OPTION	
	Type used for showConfirmDialog.	
static int	OK_OPTION	
	Return value form class method if OK is chosen.	
static String	OPTION_TYPE_PROPERTY	
	Bound property name for optionType.	
protected Object[ ]	options	
	Options to display to the user.	
static String	OPTIONS_PROPERTY	
	Bound property name for option.	
protected int	optionType	
	Option type, one of DEFAULT_OPTION, YES_NO_OPTION, YES_NO_CANCEL_OPTION or OK_CANCEL_OPTION.	
static int	PLAIN_MESSAGE	
	No icon is used.	
static int	QUESTION_MESSAGE	
	Used for questions.	
static String	SELECTION_VALUES_PROPERTY	
	Bound property name for selectionValues.	
protected Object[ ]	selectionValues	
	Array of values the user can choose from.	
static Object	UNINITIALIZED_VALUE	
	Indicates that the user has not yet selected a value.	

protected Object	value	
	Currently selected value, will be a valid option, or UNINITIALIZED_VALUE or null.	
static String	VALUE_PROPERTY	
	Bound property name for value.	
static String	WANTS_INPUT_PROPERTY	
	Bound property name for wantsInput.	
protected boolean	wantsInput	
	If true, a UI widget will be provided to the user to get input.	
static int	WARNING_MESSAGE	
	Used for warning messages.	
static int	YES_NO_CANCEL_OPTION	
	Type used for showConfirmDialog.	
static int	YES_NO_OPTION	
	Type used for showConfirmDialog.	
static int	YES_OPTION	
	Return value from class method if YES is chosen.	

Constructor Summary

JOptionPane ( )
    Creates a JOptionPane with a test message.

JOptionPane (Object message)
    Creates a instance of JOptionPane to display a message using the plain-message message type and the default options delivered by the UI.

JOptionPane (Object message, int messageType)
    Creates an instance of JOptionPane to display a message with the specified message type and the default options,

JOptionPane (Object message, int messageType, int optionType)
    Creates an instance of JOptionPane to display a message with the specified message type and options.

JOptionPane (Object message, int messageType, int optionType, Icon icon)
   Creates an instance of JOptionPane to display a message with the specified message type, options, and icon.

JOptionPane (Object message, int messageType, int optionType, Icon icon, Object[ ] options)
   Creates an instance of JOptionPane to display a message with the specified message type, icon, and options.

JOptionPane (Object message, int messageType, int optionType, Icon icon, Object[ ] options, Object initialValue)
   Creates an instance of JOptionPane to display a message with the specified message type, icon, and options, with the initially-selected option specified.

10.5. JLabel

Labels provide text information that allows the developer of software to communicate with users. Labels are defined with class JLabel a subclass of JComponent. A program using JLabel is detailed in Figure 43.

Implementation steps for a GUI with a JLabel called **label**.

1. Implement a Java program that uses JLabel in a GUI interface call **label**. Define the class head with import packages, inheritance, and variable declarations.

   ```
   import javax.swing.*;
   import java.awt.*;
   import java.awt.event.*;
   public class label extends JFrame
   { private JLabel laba; // Declare a reference.
   ```

2. Define the head of the label constructor.

   ```
   public label ( )
   {
   ```

3. Define a title for the GUI window. Create a container and set the window layout.

   ```
   super ("JLabel Example" );
   Container b = getContentPane ( );
   // Create a content pane container.
   b.setLayout (new FlowLayout ( ));
   // Create a basic layout manager.
   ```

4. Allocate a label and called laba.

   ```
   laba = new JLabel ("First Label");
   // JLabel object is instantiated.
   laba.setToolTipText ("Label Generated");
   // Display on mouse position.
   ```

5. Add the label called laba to the container.

   ```
   b.add (laba);
   ```

6. Set the size of the window.

   ```
   setSize (200, 180);
   ```

7. Display the window on the screen.

   ```
   show ( );
   ```

8. Define the tail of the label constructor

   ```
   }
   ```

9. Define the head of the Java main method with variable declarations.

   ```
   public static void main (String args [ ])
   {
   ```

10. Define and allocate a label object.

    ```
    label gen = new label ( );
    ```

11. Generate a window closing event that includes a window listener.

    ```
    gen.addWindowListener
    (
    ```

```
      new WindowAdapter ( )
      {
        public void windowClosing (WindowEvent e)
        {
          System.exit (0);
        } // End windowClosing Method
      } // End WindowAdapter
    ); // End addWindowListener
```

12. Define the tail of the Java main method.

```
    }
```

13. Define the tail of the Java label class.

```
  }
```

Implemented application using JLabel in a GUI that is saved in a file called **label.java.**

```
// JLabel example program
import javax.swing.*;
import java.awt.*;
import java.awt.event.*;
public class label extends JFrame
{ private JLabel laba; // Declare a reference.
  public label ( )
  {
    super ("JLabel Example" );
    Container b = getContentPane ( );
    // Create a content pane container.
    b.setLayout (new FlowLayout ( ));
    // Create a basic layout manager.

    laba = new JLabel ("First Label");
    // JLabel object is instantiated.
    laba.setToolTipText ("Label Generated");
    // Display on mouse position.
    b.add (laba); // Add the component to the content pane.
    setSize (200, 180); // Set the window size.
    show ( ); // Display the window on the screen.
  }
```

```
    public static void main (String args [ ])
    {
      label gen = new label ( ); // Create the label window.

      // Generate a window closing event.
      gen.addWindowListener
      (
        new WindowAdapter ( )
        {
          public void windowClosing (WindowEvent e)
          {
            System.exit (0);
          } // End windowClosing Method
        } // End WindowAdapter
      ); // End addWindowListener
    } // End main method
} // End label class
```

Figure 43. JLabel Example Program

The program declares a JLabel reference.

```
private JLabel laba;
```

A JLabel object is instantiated in the constructor. The statement

```
laba = new JLabel ("First Label");
```

creates an object with the text "First Label". The text is displayed on the label automatically.

```
laba.setToolTipText ("Label Generated");
```

uses method setToolTipText to display automatically when the user positions the mouse cursor over the label in the GUI.

10.6. Event Handling Model

The Java Graphics User Interface (GUI) is designed to support user interactions with Java programs. Interactions are implemented by associating certain program generated actions called events with user actions. Some interactions are moving the mouse, clicking the mouse, clicking a button, selecting an item from a menu, typing in a text field, and closing a window. A user interaction automatically generates an event that is sent to the program. This GUI event information is stored in an object of a class that extends **AWTEvent**. The class java.util.EventObject extends java.lang.Object, and java.awt.AWTEvent extends java.util.EventObject. In this case, java.awt.AWTEvent is an event class with subclasses ActionEvent, AdjustmentEvent, ItemEvent, and ComponentEvent. Subclasses of ComponentEvent are ContainerEvent, FocusEvent, PaintEvent, WindowEvent, and InoutEvent with subclasses KeyEvent and MouseEvent. The event types in java.awt.event are included in the Swing components. Swing has additional event types. The Swing component event types are defined in package javax.swing.event.

Event programming involves defining programs to collect the events called the **event listener** and programs to implement the actions to the event type called an **event handler**. The event listener must be registered. An event handler must be defined for each registered listener for which the GUI designer wish to interact. An event listener for a GUI event is an object of a class that implements one or more event listener from package java.awt.event and package javax.swing.event. Some event listener types in Swing and AWT components are ActionListener, AdjustmentListener, ConponentListener, FocusListener, ItemListener, KeyListener, MouseListener, MouseMotionListener, TextListener, and WindowListener that extends java.util.EventListener. Other listener types that are used in Swing components are defined in package javax.swing.event.

Interfaces define abstract methods. Any class that implements an interface must define all methods in the interface. The use of event listeners to gather actions and the use of handlers to act on the gathered actions is known as a delegation event model.

10.7. How Event Handling Works

Each event handler must be registered. Consider a text field called **mytext**. The **mytext** text field will be defined and allocated in Section 10.8 using **JTextField**. Define the event handler called **myhand**.

```
// Define and allocate listener handler called myhand.
TextFieldHandler myhand = new TextFieldHandler ( );
// Register a listener on the listenerList for the text field newtext.
newtext.addActionListener (myhand);
```

Every **JComponent** has an object of class **EventListenerList** in the package **javax.swing.event** called **listenerList** as an instance variable. All registered listeners are stored on **listenerList**.

Every **JComponent** supports several different event types, key, mouse and others. When an event occurs a unique message is send to the appropriate type event listener. The message is processed or acted on by calling the event handling method for each registered listener for that event type.

The **TextFieldHandler** object that implements **ActionListener** defined the method called **acttext** that acts on the event.

```
private class TextFieldHandler implements ActionListener
{
  public void acttext (ActionEvent e)
  {
    // Event handled code.
  } // End acttext method
} // End TextFieldHandler
```

10.8. JTextField and JPasswordField

JTextFields and **JPasswordFields** members of the **javax.swing** package are single-line areas in which text can be entered by the user from the keyboard. Text may be displayed in the JTextFields by the program at run-time. A JPasswordField displays hidden text in the field as the user input characters. The user press enter in a JTextField of a JPasswordField causes the program to generate an event. If an event listener is registered for the event type, the event is processed by the event type handler that make the JTextField or JPasswordField data available to be used by the program. The class JTextField extends class JTextComponent a package in javax.swing. Class JPasswoedField extends JTextField with several additional methods to support processing passwords.

Figure 44 details code named textpass that uses classes JTextField and JPasswordField to create and manipulate two fields. When enter is pressed in the current active field a message dialog box containing the text in the field is displayed. The password is revealed being displayed by the program.

Steps that implement a GUI using JTextField and JPasswordField are:

1. Implement a Java program that uses JTextField and JPasswordField in a GUI interface call **textpass**. Define the class head with import packages, inheritance, and variable declarations.

   ```
   // JTextField and JPasswordField example program
   import javax.swing.*;
   import java.awt.*;
   import java.awt.event.*;
   public class textpass extends JFrame
   { private JTextField mytext; // Declare a reference.
     private JPasswordField pass; // Declare a reference.
   ```

2. Define the head of the textpass constructor.

   ```
   public textpass ( )
   {
   ```

3. Define a title for the GUI window. Create a container and set the window layout.

   ```
        super ("JTestfield Example" );
        Container b = getContentPane ( );
        // Create a content pane container.
        b.setLayout (new FlowLayout ( ));
        // Create a basic layout manager.
   ```

4. Allocate a JTextField called mytext with default text and 25 visible elements.

   ```
        mytext = new JTextField ("Enter the text field ", 25);
   ```

5. Add the JTextField called mytext to the container.

   ```
        b.add (mytext); // Add the component to the content pane.
   ```

6. Allocate a JPasswordField with default text called pass.

   ```
        pass = new JPasswordField ("Hidden text");
   ```

7. Add the JPasswordFiled pass to the container.

   ```
        b.add (pass); // Add the component to the content pane.
   ```

8. Define and allocate a listener handler called myhand.

   ```
        TextFieldHandler myhand = new TextFieldHandler ( );
   ```

9. Register a listener on the listenerList for the text field mytext.

    ```
    mytext.addActionListener (myhand);
    ```

10. Register a listener on the listenerList for the text field pass.

    ```
    pass.addActionListener (myhand);
    ```

11. Set the window size.

    ```
    setSize (200, 180);
    ```

12. Display the window on the screen.

    ```
    show ( ); // Display the window on the screen.
    ```

13. Define the tail of the textpass constructor.

    ```
    }
    ```

14. Define the head of the Java main method with variable declarations.

    ```
    public static void main (String args [ ])
    {
    ```

15. Define and allocate a textpass object.

    ```
    textpass gen = new textpass ( );
    ```

16. Define a windows closing event.

    ```
    gen.addWindowListener
    (
      new WindowAdapter ( )
      {
        public void windowClosing (WindowEvent e)
        {
          System.exit (0);
        } // End windowClosing Method
      } // End WindowAdapter
    ); // End addWindowListener
    ```

17. Define the tail of the Java main method.

    ```
    } // End main method
    ```

18. Define the head of an inner class for the TextFieldHandler event handler.

    ```
    private class TextFieldHandler implements ActionListener
    {
    ```

19. Define the head of an actionPerformed method to process events.

    ```
    public void actionPerformed (ActionEvent e)
    {
    ```

20. Process the JTextField event.

    ```
    String m = " ";
    if (e.getSource ( ) == mytext)
        m = "mytext: " + e.getActionCommand ( );
    ```

21. Process the JPasswordField event.

    ```
    else if (e.getSource ( ) == pass)
      { JPasswordField pwd = (JPasswordField)e.getSource ( );
        m = "pass: " + new String (pwd.getPassword ( ));
      }
    ```

22. Output information in dialog box.

    ```
    JOptionPane.showMessageDialog (null, m);
    ```

23. Define the tail of the actionPerformed method.

    ```
    }
    ```

24. Define the tail of the TextFieldHandler method.

    ```
    }
    ```

25. Define the tail of the textpass class.

    ```
    }
    ```

Implemented application using JTextField and JPasswordField in GUI that is saved in a file called **textpass.java**.

```
// JTextField and JPasswordField example program
import javax.swing.*;
import java.awt.*;
```

```java
import java.awt.event.*;
public class textpass extends JFrame
{ private JTextField mytext; // Declare a reference.
  private JPasswordField pass; // Declare a reference.
  public textpass ( )
  {
    super ("JTestfield Example" );
    Container b = getContentPane ( );
    // Create a content pane container.
    b.setLayout (new FlowLayout ( ));
    // Create a basic layout manager.
    // Construct textfield with default text and 25 visible elements.
    mytext = new JTextField ("Enter the text field ", 25);
    b.add (mytext); // Add the component to the content pane.
    // Construct text field with default text.
    pass = new JPasswordField ("Hidden text");
    b.add (pass); // Add the component to the content pane.

    // Define and allocate listener handler called myhand.
    TextFieldHandler myhand = new TextFieldHandler ( );
    // Register a listener on the listenerList for the text field mytext.
    mytext.addActionListener (myhand);
    // Register a listener on the listenerList for the text field pass.
    pass.addActionListener (myhand);

    setSize (200, 180); // Set the window size.
    show ( ); // Display the window on the screen.
  }

  public static void main (String args [ ])
  {
    textpass gen = new textpass ( ); // Create the textpass window.

    // Generate a window closing event.
    gen.addWindowListener
    (
      new WindowAdapter ( )
      {
        public void windowClosing (WindowEvent e)
        {
          System.exit (0);
        } // End windowClosing Method
      } // End WindowAdapter
    ); // End addWindowListener
  } // End main method
```

```
    // Inner class for the event handler.
    private class TextFieldHandler implements ActionListener
    {
      public void actionPerformed (ActionEvent e)
      {
        // Event handled code.
        String m = " ";
        if (e.getSource ( ) == mytext)
          m = "mytext: " + e.getActionCommand ( );
        else if (e.getSource ( ) == pass)
          { JPasswordField pwd = (JPasswordField)e.getSource ( );
            m = "pass: " + new String (pwd.getPassword ( ));
          }
        // Output information in dialog box.
        JOptionPane.showMessageDialog (null, m);
      } // End acttext method
    } // End TextFieldHandler

} // End textpass class
```

Figure 44. JTextField and JPasswordField Input and Output

A screen view of the textpass class with textfield input and password input is:

The textfield input is **My Computer** and the password input is **pa2345**.

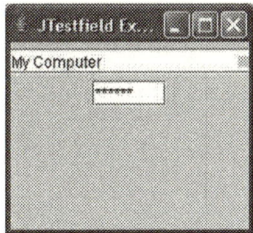

Press enter and textpass displays the hidden password.

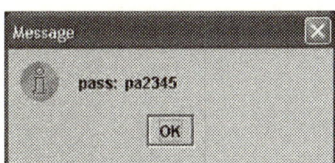

10.9. JButton

Buttons are user interface components that trigger some action in your interface when they are pressed. All button types are subclasses of **AbstractButton** a member of the **javax.swing** package.

When a user clicks a button with a mouse it generates an **ActionEvent**. Buttons are created with class **JButton**, which inherits from class **AbstractButton**. The face of a JButton is called a button label. The application in Figure 45 details the use of JButton. Event handling is performed by a single instance of inner class **ButtonHandler**.

Steps that implement a GUI using JButton are:

1. Implement a Java program that uses JButton in a GUI called **pressme**. Define the class head with import packages, inheritance, and variable declarations.

    ```
    import javax.swing.*;
    import java.awt.*;
    import java.awt.event.*;
    public class pressme extends JFrame
    { private JButton pbutton; // Declare a reference.
    ```

2. Define the head of the pressme constructor.

    ```
    public pressme ( )
    {
    ```

3. Define a title for the GUI window. Create a container and set the window layout.

    ```
        super ("JButton Example"  );
        Container b = getContentPane ( );
        // Create a content pane container.
        b.setLayout (new FlowLayout ( ));
        // Create a basic layout manager.
    ```

4. Allocate a JButton called pbutton with default text.

    ```
        // Create a plain button.
        pbutton = new JButton ("Test Button");
    ```

5. Add the JButton called pbutton to the container.

    ```
    b.add (pbutton); // Add the component to the content pane.
    ```

6. Define and allocate listener handler called myhand. Create an instance of inner class ButtonHandler.

    ```
    ButtonHandler myhand = new ButtonHandler ( );
    ```

7. Register a listener on the listenerList for the Test button.

    ```
    pbutton.addActionListener (myhand);
    ```

8. Set the window size.

    ```
    setSize (200, 180);
    ```

9. Display the window on the screen.

    ```
    show ( );
    ```

10. Define the tail of the pressme constructor.

    ```
    }
    ```

11. Define the head of the Java main method with variable declarations.

    ```
    public static void main (String args [ ])
    {
    ```

12. Define and allocate a pressme object.

    ```
    pressme gen = new pressme ( );
    ```

13. Create a window closing event.

    ```
    gen.addWindowListener
    (
      new WindowAdapter ( )
       {
         public void windowClosing (WindowEvent e)
          {
            System.exit (0);
          } // End windowClosing Method
       } // End WindowAdapter
    ); // End addWindowListener
    ```

14. Define the tail of the Java main method.

    ```
    }
    ```

15. Define the head of an inner class for the ButtonHandler event handler.

    ```
    // Inner class for the event handler.
    private class ButtonHandler implements ActionListener
    {
    ```

16. Define the head of an actionPerformed method to process events.

    ```
    public void actionPerformed (ActionEvent e)
    {
    ```

17. Process the JButton event and output information in dialog box.

    ```
    JOptionPane.showMessageDialog (null, "You pressed button: "
                          +e.getActionCommand ( ));
    ```

18. Define the tail of the actionPerformed method.

    ```
    }
    ```

19. Define the tail of the ButtonHandler method.

    ```
    }
    ```

20. Define the tail of the pressme class.

    ```
    }
    ```

Implemented application using JButton in a GUI that is saved in a file called **pressme.java**.

```
// JButton example program
import javax.swing.*;
import java.awt.*;
import java.awt.event.*;
public class pressme extends JFrame
{ private JButton pbutton; // Declare a reference.
  public pressme ( )
  {
    super ("JButton Example" );
```

```java
    Container b = getContentPane ( );
    // Create a content pane container.
    b.setLayout (new FlowLayout ( ));
    // Create a basic layout manager.
    // Create a plain button.
    pbutton = new JButton ("Test Button");
    b.add (pbutton); // Add the component to the content pane.

    // Define and allocate listener handler called myhand.
    // Create an instance of inner class ButtonHandler.
    ButtonHandler myhand = new ButtonHandler ( );
    // Register a listener on the listenerList for the Test button.
    pbutton.addActionListener (myhand);
      setSize (200, 180); // Set the window size.
      show ( ); // Display the window on the screen.
}
public static void main (String args [ ])
{
  pressme gen = new pressme ( ); // Create the pressme window.

  // Generate a window closing event.
  gen.addWindowListener
  (
    new WindowAdapter ( )
    {
      public void windowClosing (WindowEvent e)
      {
        System.exit (0);
      } // End windowClosing Method
    } // End WindowAdapter
  ); // End addWindowListener
} // End main method

// Inner class for the event handler.
private class ButtonHandler implements ActionListener
{
  public void actionPerformed (ActionEvent e)
  {
    // Event handled code.
    // Output information in dialog box.
    JOptionPane.showMessageDialog (null, "You pressed button:"
                                  +e.getActionCommand ( ));
  } // End actionPerformed method
```

```
    } // End ButtonHandler

} // End pressme class
```

Figure 45. Button and Action Event

10.10. JCheckBox

Checkboxes can be selected or deselected to provide options. Checkboxes are user interface components that have two states. The states are on or checked and off or unchecked. Checkboxes do not trigger any action in the user interface; it uses optional features of some other action. The **ItemEvent** is used by **JCheckBox**.

Class **JCheckBox** is a subclass of **JToggleButton**. The application detailed in Figure 46 uses a **JCheckBox** object to assign a variable type int named **mycheck** 200. Initially **mycheck** is set to zero. The value of the **mycheck** variable is displayed after the checkbox operation.

Steps that implement a GUI using JCheckBox are:

1. Implement a Java program that uses JButton in a GUI called **checkme**. Define the class head with import packages, inheritance, and variable declarations.

   ```
   import javax.swing.*;
   import java.awt.*;
   import java.awt.event.*;
   import java.lang.String;
   public class checkme extends JFrame
   { private JCheckBox pcheck;
     private int mycheck = 0;
   ```

2. Define the head of the checkme constructor.

   ```
   public checkme ( )
   {
   ```

3. Define a title for the GUI window. Create a container and set the window layout.

   ```
         super ("JCheckBox Example" );
         Container b = getContentPane ( );
   ```

```
// Create a content pane container.
b.setLayout (new FlowLayout ( ));
// Create a basic layout manager.
```

4. Allocate a JCkeckBox called pcheck with default text.

   ```
   pcheck = new JCheckBox ("Set 200");
   ```

5. Add the JCheckBox called pcheck to the container.

   ```
   b.add (pcheck);
   ```

6. Define and allocate listener handler called myhand. Create an instance of inner class CkeckBoxHandler.

   ```
   CheckBoxHandler myhand = new CheckBoxHandler ( );
   ```

7. Register a listener on the listenerList for the checkbox.

   ```
   pcheck.addItemListener (myhand);
   ```

8. Create a window closing event.

   ```
   addWindowListener
   (
     new WindowAdapter ( )
     {
       public void windowClosing (WindowEvent e)
       {
         System.exit (0);
       } // End windowClosing Method
     } // End WindowAdapter
   ); // End addWindowListener
   ```

9. Set the window size.

   ```
   setSize (200, 180);
   ```

10. Display the window on the screen.

    ```
    show ( );
    ```

11. Define the tail of the checkme constructor.

    ```
    }
    ```

12. Define the head of the Java main method with variable declarations.

    ```
    public static void main (String args [ ])
    {
    ```

13. Define and allocate a checkme object.

    ```
    new checkme ( );
    ```

14. Define the tail of the Java main method.

    ```
    }
    ```

15. Define the head of an inner class for the CheckBoxHandler event handler.

    ```
    private class CheckBoxHandler implements ItemListener
    {
    ```

16. Define the head of an itemStateChanged method to process events.

    ```
    public void itemStateChanged (ItemEvent e)
    {
       String m = "Variable value is ";
    ```

17. Process the JCheckBox events.

    ```
    if (e.getSource ( ) == pcheck)
      if (e.getStateChange ( ) == ItemEvent.SELECTED)
        mycheck = 200;
      else
        mycheck = 45;
    ```

18. Output information in dialog box.

    ```
    JOptionPane.showMessageDialog (null, m+mycheck);//+mm);
    ```

19. Define the tail of the itemStateChange method.

    ```
    }
    ```

20. Define the tail of the CheckBoxHandler method.

    ```
    }
    ```

21. Define the tail of the checkme class.

```
}
```

Implemented application using JCheckBox in a GUI that is saved in a file called **checkme.java**.

```java
// JCheckBox example program
import javax.swing.*;
import java.awt.*;
import java.awt.event.*;
import java.lang.String;
public class checkme extends JFrame
{ private JCheckBox pcheck; // Declare a reference.
  private int mycheck = 0;
  public checkme ( )
  {
    super ("JCheckBox Example" );
    Container b = getContentPane ( );
    // Create a content pane container.
    b.setLayout (new FlowLayout ( ));
    // Create a basic layout manager.
    // Create a checkbox object.
    pcheck = new JCheckBox ("Set 200");
    b.add (pcheck); // Add the component to the content pane.

    // Define and allocate listener handler called myhand.
    // Create an instance of inner class CheckBoxHandler.
    CheckBoxHandler myhand = new CheckBoxHandler ( );
    // Register a listener on the listenerList for the checkbox.
    pcheck.addItemListener (myhand);

    // Generate a window closing event.
    addWindowListener
    (
      new WindowAdapter ( )
      {
        public void windowClosing (WindowEvent e)
        {
          System.exit (0);
        } // End windowClosing Method
      } // End WindowAdapter
    ); // End addWindowListener
```

```
      setSize (200, 180); // Set the window size.
      show ( ); // Display the window on the screen.
   }

   public static void main (String args [ ])
   {
     new checkme ( ); // Create the checkme window.
   } // End main method

   // Inner class for the event handler.
   private class CheckBoxHandler implements ItemListener
   {
     public void itemStateChanged (ItemEvent e)
     {
       // Event handled code.
       String m = "Variable value is ";
       if (e.getSource ( ) == pcheck)
         if (e.getStateChange ( ) == ItemEvent.SELECTED)
           mycheck = 200;
         else
           mycheck = 45;
       //String mm =(String)mycheck;
       // Output information in dialog box.
       JOptionPane.showMessageDialog (null, m+mycheck);//+mm);
     } // End actchk method
   } // End CheckBoxHandler

} // End checkme class
```

Figure 46. Checkbox Operation

Ascreen view of the checkme class execution is:

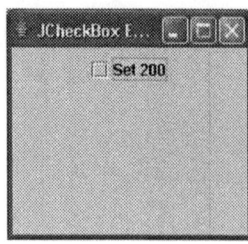

Click the check box.

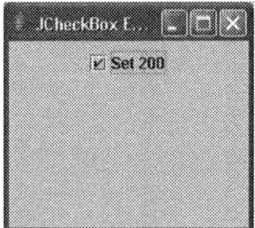

Display the variable value of the checked box.

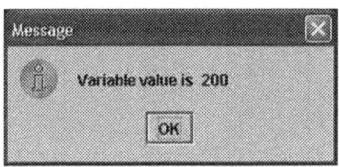

10.11. JComboBox

A combo box or a drop-down list is provided from which the user can make a selection. Class **JComboBox** is used to implement combo boxes, which inherits from the class **JComponent**. **JComboBox**es generate **ItemEvent**s like the **JCheckBox**es.

The application of Figure 47 uses JComboBox to provide a list of three relational operator names. A relational operator name is selected; the corresponding character relational operator is displayed in a JOptionPane dialog box.

Steps that implement a GUI using JComboBox are:

1. Implement a Java program that uses JComboBox in a GUI called **combob**. Define the class head with import packages, inheritance, and variable declarations.

    ```
    import javax.swing.*;
    import java.awt.*;
    import java.awt.event.*;
    public class combob extends JFrame
    ```

```
{ private JComboBox pcombo; // Declare a reference.
  private JLabel label;
  private String clist [ ] = {"Equal", "Less Than", "Greater Than"};
  private String tlist [ ] = {"=", "<", ">"};
```

2. Define the head of the combob constructor.

   ```
   public combob ( )
   {
   ```

3. Define a title for the GUI window. Create a container and set the window layout.

   ```
   super ("JComboBox Example" );
   Container b = getContentPane ( );
   // Create a content pane container.
   b.setLayout (new FlowLayout ( ));
   // Create a basic layout manager.
   ```

4. Allocate a JComboBox called pcombo.

   ```
   pcombo = new JComboBox (clist);
   pcombo.setMaximumRowCount (3);
   ```

5. Define the head of the addItemListener method.

   ```
   pcombo.addItemListener (new ItemListener ( )
   {
   ```

6. Define the head of the itemStateChanged method.

   ```
   public void itemStateChanged (ItemEvent e)
   {
   ```

7. Output the selected result.

   ```
   JOptionPane.showMessageDialog (null, "The Selected Result
   is: " + tlist [pcombo.getSelectedIndex ( )]);
   ```

8. Define the tail of the itemStateChanged method.

   ```
   }
   ```

9. Define the tail of the addItemListener method.

   ```
       }
   );
   ```

10. Add the pcombo to the container.

    ```
    b.add (pcombo);
    ```

11. Allocate a JLabel called label.

    ```
    label = new JLabel (tlist [0]);
    ```

12. Add the label to the container.

    ```
    b.add (label);
    ```

13. Set the window size.

    ```
    setSize (300, 180);
    ```

14. Display the window on the screen.

    ```
    show ( );
    ```

15. Define the tail of the combob constructor.

    ```
    }
    ```

16. Define the head of the Java main method with variable declarations.

    ```
    public static void main (String args [ ])
    {
    ```

17. Define and allocate a combob object.

    ```
    combob gen = new combob ( );
    ```

18. Create a window closing event.

    ```
    gen.addWindowListener
    (
       new WindowAdapter ( )
       {
          public void windowClosing (WindowEvent e)
    ```

```
            {
               System.exit (0);
            } // End windowClosing Method
         } // End WindowAdapter
      ); // End addWindowListener
```

19. Define the tail of the Java main method.

    ```
    }
    ```

20. Define the tail of the combob class.

    ```
    }
    ```

Implemented application using JComboBox in a GUI that is saved in a file called **combob.java**.

```
// JComboBox example program
import javax.swing.*;
import java.awt.*;
import java.awt.event.*;
public class combob extends JFrame
{ private JComboBox pcombo; // Declare a reference.
  private JLabel label;
  private String clist [ ] = {"Equal", "Less Than", "Greater Than"};
  private String tlist [ ] = {"=", "<", ">"};

  public combob ( )
  {
  super ("JComboBox Example" );
    Container b = getContentPane ( );
    // Create a content pane container.
    b.setLayout (new FlowLayout ( ));
    // Create a basic layout manager.
    // Create a combo box object.
    pcombo = new JComboBox (clist);
    pcombo.setMaximumRowCount (3);

    pcombo.addItemListener (new ItemListener ( )
       {
          public void itemStateChanged (ItemEvent e)
          {
             JOptionPane.showMessageDialog (null, "The Selected Result
             is:" +tlist [pcombo.getSelectedIndex ( )]);
          }
```

```
      }
    );

    b.add (pcombo);
    label = new JLabel (tlist [0]);
    b.add (label);
    setSize (300, 180); // Set the window size.
    show ( ); // Display the window on the screen.
  }

  public static void main (String args [ ])
  {
    combob gen = new combob ( ); // Create the combome window.

    // Generate a window closing event.
    gen.addWindowListener
    (
      new WindowAdapter ( )
      {
        public void windowClosing (WindowEvent e)
        {
          System.exit (0);
        } // End windowClosing Method
      } // End WindowAdapter
    ); // End addWindowListener

  } // End main method

} // End combob class
```

Figure 47. Combo Box Operation

A screen view of the comcoc class execution is:

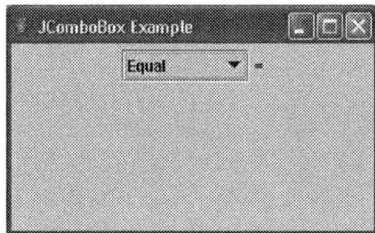

Select or click on **Less Than**.

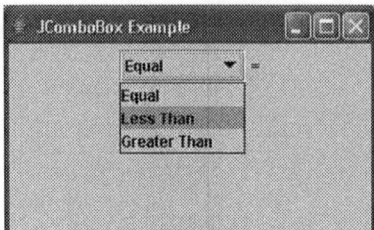

The selected result is displayed in a dialog box.

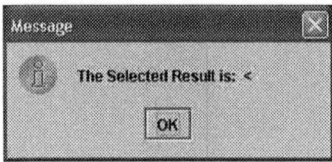

10.12. Mouse Event Handling

Public interface **MouseListener** extends **EventListener** the listener interface for receiving mouse events press, release, click, enter, and exit on a component. To track mouse moves and mouse drags, use the **MouseMotionListener**.

Each mouse event handling methods takes a **MouseEvent** object as its argument. A **MouseEvent** object contains information about the mouse event that occurred. This includes the coordinates of the location where the event occurred. **MouseListener** and **MouseMotionListener** methods are called automatically when the mouse interacts with a Component registered listener object. The class that processes a mouse event either implements this interface and all the methods it contains or extends the abstract **MouseAdapter** class by overriding methods.

The listener object created from that class is then registered with a component using the component's **addMouseListener** method. A mouse event is generated when the mouse is pressed, released, or clicked. Clicked is defined by a mouse key pressed and released within a time interval that defines a click. A mouse event is also generated when the mouse cursor enters or leaves a component. When a mouse event occurs, the relevant method in the registered listener object is invoked, and the **MouseEvent** is passed to it. A mouse methods summary is detailed in Figure 48.

Method	Description
void mouseClicked(MouseEvent e)	Invoked when the mouse button has been clicked (pressed and released) on a component.
void mouseEntered(MouseEvent e)	Invoked when the mouse enters a component.
void mouseExited(MouseEvent e)	Invoked when the mouse exits a component.
void mousePressed(MouseEvent e)	Invoked when a mouse button has been pressed on a component.
void mouseReleased(MouseEvent e)	Invoked when a mouse button has been released on a component.
void mouseDragged(MouseEvent e)	Invoked when a mouse button is pressed on a component and then dragged.
void mouseMoved(MouseEvent e)	Invoked when the mouse cursor has been moved onto a component but no buttons have been pushed.

Figure 48. Mouse Method Summary

MouseMotionListener is invoked when a mouse button is pressed on a **Component** and then dragged. **MOUSE_DRAGGED** events will continue to be delivered to the component where the drag originated until the mouse button is released.

mouseClicked is invoked when the mouse button has been clicked (pressed and released) on a component. This indicates that a mouse action occurred in a component. A mouse action is considered to occur in a particular component if and only if the mouse cursor is over the unobscured part of the component's bounds when the action happens. Component bounds can be obscured by the visible component's children or by a menu or by a top-level window. This event is used both for mouse events click, enter, exit, and mouse motion events moves and drags.

This low-level event is generated by a component object for:

Mouse Events

- a mouse button is pressed
- a mouse button is released
- a mouse button is clicked (pressed and released)
- the mouse cursor enters the unobscured part of component's geometry
- the mouse cursor exits the unobscured part of component's geometry
- Mouse Motion Events
- the mouse is moved
- the mouse is dragged

A **MouseEvent** object is passed to every **MouseListener** or **MouseAdapter** object which is registered to receive the mouse events using the component's **addMouseListener** method. **MouseAdapter** objects implement the **MouseListener** interface. Each such listener object gets a **MouseEvent** containing the mouse event.

A **MouseEvent** object is also passed to every **MouseMotionListener** or **MouseMotionAdapter** object which is registered to receive mouse motion events using the component's **addMouseMotionListener** method. **MouseMotionAdapter** objects implement the **MouseMotionListener** interface. Each such listener object gets a **MouseEvent** containing the mouse motion event.

When a mouse button is clicked, events are generated and sent to the registered **MouseListeners**. The state of modal keys can be retrieved using **InputEvent.getModifiers ( )** and **InputEvent.getModifiersEx ( )**. The button mask returned by **InputEvent.getModifiers ( )** reflects only the button that changed state, not the current state of all buttons. Due to overlap in the values of ALT_MASK/BUTTON2_MASK and META_MASK/BUTTON3_MASK, this is not always true for mouse events involving modifier keys. To get the state of all buttons and modifier keys, use **InputEvent.getModifiersEx ( )**. The button which has changed state is returned by **getButton ( )**

For example, if the first mouse button is pressed, events are sent in the following order:

id	modifiers	button
MOUSE_PRESSED:	BUTTON1_MASK	BUTTON1
MOUSE_RELEASED:	BUTTON1_MASK	BUTTON1
MOUSE_CLICKED:	BUTTON1_MASK	BUTTON1

A **tracker** application using **MouseListener** and **MouseMotionListener** methods is detailed in Figure 49. The application implements both interfaces and it can listen to its own mouse events.

Steps that implement MouseListener and MouseMotionListener are:

1. Implement a Java program that implements MouseListener and MouseMotionListener to trace the coordinates of the mouse movement called **tracker**. Define the class head with import packages and variable declarations.

   ```
   import javax.swing.*;
   import java.awt.*;
   import java.awt.event.*;
   public class tracker extends JFrame implements MouseListener,
   MouseMotionListener
   { private JLabel status; // Declare a reference.
   ```

2. Define the head of the tracker constructor.

   ```
   public tracker ( )
   {
   ```

3. Define a title for the GUI window and allocate a JLabel called status. Create a container and set the window layout.

   ```
   super ("Mouse Events Example" );
   status = new JLabel ( );
   Container b = getContentPane ( );
   // Create a content pane container.
   b.add (status, BorderLayout.SOUTH);
   // Create a basic layout manager.
   ```

4. Define an application that listens to its own mouse events.

   ```
   addMouseListener (this);
   addMouseMotionListener (this);
   ```

5. Set the window size.

   ```
   setSize (200, 180);
   ```

6. Display the window on the screen.

   ```
   show ( );
   ```

7. Define the tail of the tracker constructor.

   ```
   }
   ```

8. Define the MouseListener event handlers.

   ```
   public void mouseClicked (MouseEvent e)
   {
     status.setText ("Clicked Coordinate: (" + e.getX ( ) + ", " +
                 e.getY ( ) + ")");
   }

   public void mousePressed (MouseEvent e)
   {
     status.setText ("Pressed Coordinate: (" + e.getX ( ) + ", " +
                 e.getY ( ) + ")");
   }

   public void mouseReleased (MouseEvent e)
   {
     status.setText ("Released Coordinate: (" + e.getX ( ) + ", " +
                 e.getY ( ) + ")");
   }

   public void mouseEntered (MouseEvent e)
   {
     status.setText ("Mouse is in window");
   }

   public void mouseExited (MouseEvent e)
   {
     status.setText ("Mouse is outside window");
   }

   // MouseModionListener event handlers
   public void mouseDragged (MouseEvent e)
   {
   ```

```
   status.setText ("Dragged Coordinate at: (" + e.getX ( ) + ", "
                 + e.getY ( ) + ")");
}

public void mouseMoved (MouseEvent e)
{
   status.setText ("Moved Coordinate: (" + e.getX ( ) + ", " +
                 e.getY ( ) + ")");
}

public static void main (String args [ ])
{
   tracker gen = new tracker ( );
```

9. Create a window closing event.

```
gen.addWindowListener
(
   new WindowAdapter ( )
   {
      public void windowClosing (WindowEvent e)
      {
         System.exit (0);
      } // End windowClosing Method
   } // End WindowAdapter
); // End addWindowListener
```

10. Define the tail of the Java main method.

```
   }
```

11. Define the tail of the tracker class

```
}
```

Implemented application using MouseListener and MouseMotionListener that is saved in a file called **tracker.java**.

```
// MouseLiatener and MouseMotionListener example program
import javax.swing.*;
import java.awt.*;
import java.awt.event.*;
public class tracker extends JFrame implements MouseListener,
MouseMotionListener
```

```java
{ private JLabel status; // Declare a reference.
  public tracker ( )
  {
    super ("Mouse Events Example" );
    status = new JLabel ( );
    Container b = getContentPane ( );
    // Create a content pane container.
    b.add (status, BorderLayout.SOUTH);
    // Create a basic layout manager.
    // Create a label.
    status = new JLabel ( );
    // Application listens to its own mouse events
    addMouseListener (this);
    addMouseMotionListener (this);

    setSize (200, 180); // Set the window size.
    show ( ); // Display the window on the screen.
  }

  // MouseListener event handler
  public void mouseClicked (MouseEvent e)
  {
    status.setText ("Clicked Coordinate: (" + e.getX ( ) + ", " +
                e.getY ( ) + ")");
  }

  public void mousePressed (MouseEvent e)
  {
    status.setText ("Pressed Coordinate: (" + e.getX ( ) + ", " +
                e.getY ( ) + ")");
  }

  public void mouseReleased (MouseEvent e)
  {
    status.setText ("Released Coordinate: (" + e.getX ( ) + ", " +
                e.getY ( ) + ")");
  }

  public void mouseEntered (MouseEvent e)
  {
    status.setText ("Mouse is in window");
  }
```

```java
public void mouseExited (MouseEvent e)
{
  status.setText ("Mouse is outside window");
}

// MouseModionListener event handlers
public void mouseDragged (MouseEvent e)
{
  status.setText ("Dragged Coordinate at: (" + e.getX ( ) + ", "
              + e.getY ( ) + ")");
}

public void mouseMoved (MouseEvent e)
{
  status.setText ("Moved Coordinate: (" + e.getX ( ) + ", " +
              e.getY ( ) + ")");
}

public static void main (String args [ ])
{
  tracker gen = new tracker ( ); // Create the tracker window.

  // Generate a window closing event.
  gen.addWindowListener
  (
    new WindowAdapter ( )
    {
      public void windowClosing (WindowEvent e)
      {
        System.exit (0);
      } // End windowClosing Method
    } // End WindowAdapter
  ); // End addWindowListener

} // End main method

} // End tracker class
```

Figure 49. Mouse Event Handling

10.13. Keyboard Event Handling

Keyboard event handling is managed in a class that implements **KeyListener**. The **KeyListener** interface is initiated to track user actions from the keyboard. The **KeyListener** interface contains methods **keyPressed ( )**, **keyTyped ( )**, and **keyReleased ( )**. In most cases, the fact that a key is pressed is not of interest. An important user action on the keyboard is the key release that can be placed in the **keyReleased ( )** method.

A keyboard character can be tracked with the **keyTyped ( )**. This works if the key pressed returns a character. A function key pressed does not return a character and is called an action key. The **keyTyped ( )** method is not executed for action key.

The **board** application detailed in Figure 50 implements **KeyListener**.

Steps that implement a GUI using LeyListener are:

1. Implement a Java program that uses KeyListener in a GUI called **board**. Define the class head with import packages, inheritance, and variable declarations.

    ```
    import javax.swing.*;
    import java.awt.*;
    import java.awt.event.*;
    public class board extends JFrame implements KeyListener
    {
    ```

2. Define the head of the board class constructor.

    ```
    // Class board constructor.
    public board ( )
    {
    ```

3. Set the title of the GUI window and make addKeyListener reference itself.

    ```
    // Place a title in the window title bar.
    setTitle ("Key Frame");
    addKeyListener (this);
    ```

4. Define the tail of the board class constructor.

    ```
    }
    ```

5. Define the head of the keyPressed abstract method. When a key is pressed display Pressed.

    ```
    public void keyPressed (KeyEvent e)
    {
    ```

6. Display the message Pressed in a dialog box.

    ```
    JOptionPane.showMessageDialog (null, "Pressed");
    ```

7. Define the tail of the keyPressed method.

    ```
    }
    ```

8. Define the head of the keyTyped abstract method. When a non-action key is pressed display Typed.

    ```
    public void keyTyped (KeyEvent e)
    {
    ```

9. Display the message Typed in a dialog box.

    ```
    JOptionPane.showMessageDialog (null, "Typed");
    ```

10. Define the tail of the keyTyped method.

    ```
    }
    ```

11. Define the head of the keyReleased abstract method. When a key is released display Released.

    ```
    public void keyReleased (KeyEvent e)
    {
    ```

12. Display the message Released in a dialog box.

    ```
    JOptionPane.showMessageDialog (null, "Released");
    ```

13. Define the tail of the keyReleased method.

    ```
    }
    ```

14. Define the head of the Java main method.

    ```
    public static void main (String [ ] args)
    {
    ```

15. Create a board object called gen.

    ```
    board gen = new board ( );
    ```

16. Set the window size.

    ```
    gen.setSize (250, 50);
    ```

17. Make the window visible and display it on the screen.

    ```
    gen.setVisible (true);
    ```

18. Define the tail of the Java main method.

    ```
    }
    ```

19. Define the tail of the board class.

    ```
    }
    ```

Implemented application using KeyListener in a GUI that is saved in a file called **board.java**.

```
// KeyListener example program
import javax.swing.*;
import java.awt.*;
import java.awt.event.*;
public class board extends JFrame implements KeyListener
{
  // Class board constructor.
  public board ( )
  {
    // Place a title in the window title bar.
    setTitle ("Key Frame");
    addKeyListener (this);
  }

  // keyPressed abstract method. When a key is pressed display Pressed.
  public void keyPressed (KeyEvent e)
  {
    JOptionPane.showMessageDialog (null, "Pressed");
  }
```

```
// keyTyped abstract method. When a non-action key is pressed
// display Typed.
public void keyTyped (KeyEvent e)
{
   JOptionPane.showMessageDialog (null, "Typed");
}

// keyReleased abstract method. When a key is released display Released.
public void keyReleased (KeyEvent e)
{
   JOptionPane.showMessageDialog (null, "Released");
}

// Instantiate the class board and Size the window.
public static void main (String [ ] args)
{
   board gen = new board ( );
   gen.setSize (250, 50);
   gen.setVisible (true);
} // End main Method
} // End board Class
```

Figure 50. Implement KeyListener

10.14. Layout Managers

A **layout manager** is an object that governs how components are arranged in a container. It determines the size and position of each component in the container. Every container has a default layout manager that can be replaced.

The container layout manager is consulted for every change in the visual appearance of component in a container. When the size of a container is adjusted, the layout manager is consulted to determine how all of the components in the container should appear in the resized container. Every time a new component is added to a container, the layout manager determines how the addition affects all of the existing components. Figure 51 details several predefined layout managers provided by the Java standard class library.

Layout Manager	Description
Border Layout	Organizes components into areas North, South, East, West, and Center.
Box Layout	Organizes components into a single row or column.
Card Layout	Organizes components into one area such that only one is visible at a time.
Flow Layout	Organizes components from left to right, starting new rows as necessary,
Grid Layout	Organizes components into a grid of rows and columns.
GridBag Layout	Organizes components into a grid of cells, allowing components to span more than one cell.

Figure 51. Several Java Predefined Layout Managers

In some layout managers, the order in which you add components affects their positioning in the container. There are other ways that provide more specific control with in the layout manager. Features and characteristics of various Java layout managers empower developers to produce good GUI products.

10.14.1. FlowLayout

The FlowLayout class is the most basic of layouts. Components are added to the panel one at a time, row by row. If a component doesn't fit on a row, it is wrapped onto the next row. This layout has a row alignment. The default is aligned centered. Create a basic flow layout with centered alignment in your panel's initialization:

```
setLayout (new FlowLayout ( ));
```

To create a flow layout with an alignment right, add FlowLayout.RIGHT or left FlowLayout.LEFT class variable as an argument:

```
setLayout (new FlowLayout (FlowLayout.LEFT));
```

Horizontal and vertical gap values may be used in flow layouts. The gap is the number of pixels between components in a panel. The default horizontal and vertical gap values are three pixels. Add integer arguments to the flow layout constructor to increase the gap 10 points in the horizontal and vertical:

```
setLayout (new FlowLayout (FlowLayout.LEFT), 10, 10);
```

Figure 52 details an application **flow** to lay out buttons in a panel.

Steps that implement a GUI using FlowLayout are:

1. Implement a Java program that uses FlowLayout in a GUI called **flow**. Define the class head with import packages, inheritance, and variable declarations.
   ```
   import java.awt.*;
   import javax.swing.*;
   public class flow extends JApplet
   {
   ```

2. Define the head of the Java applet init ( ) method.
   ```
   public void init ( )
   {
   ```

3. Check access to system event queue message seen in some browsers.
   ```
   getRootPane( ).putClientProperty("defeatSystemEventQueueCheck",
                         Boolean.TRUE);
   ```

4. Set the layout of the panel.
   ```
   getContentPane ( ).setLayout (null);
   ```

5. Set the window size.
   ```
   setSize (426, 266);
   ```

6. Set the lable on a button.
   ```
   button1.setLabel ("First");
   ```

7. Add the button to the panel.
   ```
   getContentPane ( ).add (button1);
   ```

8. Set the background color
   ```
   button1.setBackground (java.awt.Color.lightGray);
   ```

9. Set the bounds on the button.

```
button1.setBounds (72, 48, 93, 50);
button2.setLabel ("Second");
getContentPane ( ).add (button2);
button2.setBackground (java.awt.Color.lightGray);
button2.setBounds (240, 48, 110, 48);
button3.setLabel ("Third");
getContentPane ( ).add (button3);
button3.setBackground (java.awt.Color.lightGray);
button3.setBounds (72, 144, 96, 48);
button4.setLabel ("Fourth");
getContentPane ( ).add (button4);
button4.setBackground (java.awt.Color.lightGray);
button4.setBounds (240, 144, 108, 48);
```

10. Define the tail of the init method.

```
}
```

11. Define and allocate buttons.

```
java.awt.Button button1 = new java.awt.Button ( );
java.awt.Button button2 = new java.awt.Button ( );
java.awt.Button button3 = new java.awt.Button ( );
java.awt.Button button4 = new java.awt.Button ( );
```

12. Define the tail of the flow class.

```
}
```

Implemented application using FlowLayout in a GUI that is saved in a file called **flow.java**.

```
// Flow Layout Example Program
import java.awt.*;
import javax.swing.*;
public class flow extends JApplet
{
  public void init ( )
   {
    // This line prevents the "Swing: checked access to system
       event queue"
    // message seen in some browsers.
    getRootPane( ).putClientProperty("defeatSystemEventQueueCheck",
                          Boolean.TRUE);
```

```
        getContentPane ( ).setLayout (null);
        setSize (426, 266);
        button1.setLabel ("First");
        getContentPane ( ).add (button1);
        button1.setBackground (java.awt.Color.lightGray);
        button1.setBounds (72, 48, 93, 50);
        button2.setLabel ("Second");
        getContentPane ( ).add (button2);
        button2.setBackground (java.awt.Color.lightGray);
        button2.setBounds (240, 48, 110, 48);
        button3.setLabel ("Third");
        getContentPane ( ).add (button3);
        button3.setBackground (java.awt.Color.lightGray);
        button3.setBounds (72, 144, 96, 48);
        button4.setLabel ("Fourth");
        getContentPane ( ).add (button4);
        button4.setBackground (java.awt.Color.lightGray);
        button4.setBounds (240, 144, 108, 48);
    }

    // Declare controls
    java.awt.Button button1 = new java.awt.Button ( );
    java.awt.Button button2 = new java.awt.Button ( );
    java.awt.Button button3 = new java.awt.Button ( );
    java.awt.Button button4 = new java.awt.Button ( );
}
```

Figure 52. Flow Layout Buttons in a Panel

10.14.2. BorderLayout

Border layouts behave differently from flow layouts. Components are added to a panel with a placement defined as a geographic direction north, south, east, west, and center.

To use a border layout, create it when the panel is defined with:

```
setLayout (new BorderLayout ( ));
```

Add individual components with a special add ( ) method. The first argument to add ( ) is a string indicating the position of the component within the layout:

```
add ("West", new TextField ("Side", 50));
```

Figure 53 details an application **border** to lay out buttons in a panel.

Steps that implement a GUI using BorderLayout are:

1. Implement a Java program that uses BorderLayout in a GUI called **border**. Define the class head with import packages, inheritance, and variable declarations.

    ```
    import java.applet.*;
    import javax.swing.*;
    import java.awt.*;
    import java.awt.event.*;
    public class border extends Applet
    { private Button nor = new Button ("North Border");
      private Button sou = new Button ("South Border");
      private Button eas = new Button ("East Border");
      private Button wes = new Button ("West Border");
      private Button cen = new Button ("Center All");
    ```

2. Define the head of the Java applet init ( ) method.

    ```
    public void init ( )
    {
    ```

3. Set the layout for s BorderLayout.

    ```
        setLayout (new BorderLayout ( ));
    ```

4. Add the Buttons to the BorderLayout.

    ```
        add (nor, "North");
        add (sou, "South");
        add (eas, "East");
        add (wes, "West");
        add (cen, "Center");
    ```

5. Define the tail of the init method.

    ```
    }
    ```

6. Define the tail of the border class.

    ```
    }
    ```

Implemented application using BorderLayout in a GUI that is saved in a file called **border.java**.

```
// Border Layout example program
import java.applet.*;
import javax.swing.*;
import java.awt.*;
import java.awt.event.*;

public class border extends Applet
{ private Button nor = new Button ("North Border");
  private Button sou = new Button ("South Border");
  private Button eas = new Button ("East Border");
  private Button wes = new Button ("West Border");
  private Button cen = new Button ("Center All");

  public void init ( )
  {
    setLayout (new BorderLayout ( ));
    add (nor, "North");
    add (sou, "South");
    add (eas, "East");
    add (wes, "West");
    add (cen, "Center");
  }
}
```

Figure 53. Border Layout Buttons in a Panel

10.14.3. GridLayout

The **GridLayout** class is used to arrange Components into equal rows and columns. The Container surface is divided into the number of rows and columns when the **GridLayout** is created. For example, the statement

```
setLayout (new GridLayout (6, 4);
```

establishes a GridLayout with six horizontal rows and four vertical columns.

10.15. Panels

FlowLayout and BorderLayout managers provide a limited number of screen arrangements. The number of possible Component arrangements can be increased using the Panel class. A Panel is similar to a Window in that a Panel is a surface on which Components are placed. A panel is a Container, which means that it can contain other Components.

When you create a Panel object, you can use one of two constructors:

```
Panel ( ); // Use the default layout manager FlowLayout.

Panel (LayoutManager lay); // lay is the specified layout manager.
```

Figure 54 details an application **pan** that implements a JPanel.

Steps that implement a GUI using JPanel are:

1. Implement a Java program that uses JPanel in a GUI called **pan**. Define the class head with import packages, inheritance, and variable declarations.

   ```
   import javax.swing.*;
   import java.awt.*;
   import java.awt.event.*;
   public class pan extends JFrame
   { private JPanel bpanel;
     private JButton butt [ ];
   ```

2. Define the head of the pan class constructor.

   ```
   public pan ( )
   {
   ```

3. Define a title for the window and a container.

   ```
   super ("Panel Example" );
   Container b = getContentPane ( );
   ```

4. Allocate a JPanel called bpanel.

   ```
   bpanel = new JPanel ( );
   ```

5. Allocate a JButton called butt.

   ```
   butt = new JButton [5];
   ```

6. Set the layout for a GridLayout.

    ```
    bpanel.setLayout (new GridLayout (1, butt.length));
    ```

7. Add the JButtons to the JPanel.

    ```
    for (int j = 0; j < butt.length; j++)
    { butt [j] = new JButton ("Button " + (j + 1));
      bpanel.add (butt [j]);
    }
    ```

8. Add the JPanel to a BorderLayout.

    ```
    b.add (bpanel, BorderLayout.SOUTH);
    ```

9. Set the window size.

    ```
    setSize (200, 180);
    ```

10. Display the window on the screen.

    ```
    show ( );
    ```

11. Define the tail of the pan constructor method.

    ```
    }
    ```

12. Define the head of the Java main method.

    ```
    public static void main (String args [ ])
    {
    ```

13. Create a panel object called gen.

    ```
    pan gen = new pan ( ); // Create the pan window.
    ```

14. Create a window closing event.

    ```
    gen.addWindowListener
    (
      new WindowAdapter ( )
      {
        public void windowClosing (WindowEvent e)
        {
          System.exit (0);
    ```

```
        } // End windowClosing Method
      } // End WindowAdapter
    ); // End addWindowListener
```

15. Define the tail of the Java main method.

    ```
    }
    ```

16. Define the tail of the pan class.

    ```
    }
    ```

Implemented application using JPanel in a GUI that is saved in a file called pan.java.

```
// JPanel example program
import javax.swing.*;
import java.awt.*;
import java.awt.event.*;
public class pan extends JFrame
{ private JPanel bpanel; // Declare a reference.
  private JButton butt [ ];
  public pan ( )
  {
    super ("Panel Example" );
    Container b = getContentPane ( );
    // Create a content pane container.

    bpanel = new JPanel ( );
    butt = new JButton [5];

    bpanel.setLayout (new GridLayout (1, butt.length));

    for (int j = 0; j < butt.length; j++)
    { butt [j] = new JButton ("Button " + (j + 1));
      bpanel.add (butt [j]);
    }

    b.add (bpanel, BorderLayout.SOUTH);

    setSize (200, 180); // Set the window size.
    show ( ); // Display the window on the screen.
  }
```

```
public static void main (String args [ ])
{
  pan gen = new pan ( ); // Create the pan window.

  // Generate a window closing event.
  gen.addWindowListener
  (
    new WindowAdapter ( )
    {
      public void windowClosing (WindowEvent e)
      {
        System.exit (0);
      } // End windowClosing Method
    } // End WindowAdapter
  ); // End addWindowListener

} // End main method
} // End pan class
```

Figure 54. Panel Application

10.16. Exercises

1. Write a program to meet the requirements:

    Create a frame with FlowLayout.
    Create two panels and add the panels to the frame.
    Each panel contains three buttons. The panel uses FlowLayout.

2. Write a program to display the mouse position when the mouse is pressed.

3. Write a program that read input from a text field and output the text in a different text field.

4. Using **TextFields**, write an applet that requests a name, street address, city name, and zip code from a user. A **submit** button collects all the data from the text fields, stores it in an array, and asks for data for another person. A **quit** button ends the session and displays all or the information within a text area of the applet.

5. Write a GUI that can be used with a collection of CDs. Enter the CD data name, artist, year, and price using the GUI, display the CD, and store it in

array of CDs. Add **view** and **store** control buttons that allow you to retrieve all the data for a particular CD given its title, calculate the total value of your collection, view all the CDs by a particular artist, and delete a CD from your collection.

6. Write a GUI application to receive multiple lines of text from the user and write it in a text file named **myarea.dat.**

11
Multithreading

11.1. Introduction

A thread is the flow of execution of one set of program statements from the start to the end statement. The program executes statement by statement as a single program.

Single-thread programs contain statements that executes at a high rate of speed on fast central processing units (CPU)s. The CPU executes one statement at a time regardless of its speed. A computer with more than one CPU can execute more that one statement at the same time.

The Java programming language allows you to **launch** or start multiple threads. Java supports the launch of multiple threads on machines independent of the processor speed. The act of launching and managing more than one thread is known as **multithreading**.

Multiple threads executing on a computer with one CPU share the same CPU. A small time slice is devoted to each thread until the end of process. A CPU never perform more than one task at the same instant. It performs a small piece of one task, end then a small piece of another task.

Programmers use multithreading to increase the performance of their programs. In general, multithreading programs run faster and supports good user friendly GUIs. Threads can be launched in response to user interactions with the GUI. An animation can execute on in one window as the user interact with a GUI in other windows. A file can be read on one thread while the CPU is serving other user activities.

11.2. The Thread Class

Threads can be created by extending class **Thread** defined in the **java.lang** package. The class Thread contains a method named **run ( )** that may be overwritten to tell the system how to execute the Thread.

```
public void run ( )
```

The constructor

```
public Thread (String tname)
```

constructs a Thread object whose name is **tname**. The constructor

```
public Thread ( )
```

constructs a Thread whose name is "Thread-" concatenated with a number, like Thread-1, Thread-2, and Thread-3.

A program launches a thread's execution by calling the thread's **start ( )** method which causes the run ( ) method to be invoked.

```
public void start ( )
```

The stop ( ) method stops the thread.

```
public void stop ( )
```

Threads can be suspended by invoking the suspend ( ) method.

```
public void suspend ( )
```

Other Thread methods are:

Method	Description
public static void sleep (long mille) throws InterruptedException	Sleep the object for mille seconds.
public static Boolean interrupted ( )	Tests whether the current thread has been interrupted.
public Boolean isAlive ( )	Tests whether the thread is currently running.
public void setPriority (int h)	Sets priority h ranging from 1 to 10 for this thread.

These methods are used to manage the five Thread states new, ready, running, inactive, or finished.

For example, Figure 55 details **mthread** multiple threads printing at different intervals.

Steps that implement a multiple thread application are:

1. Implement a Java program that uses JPanel in a GUI called **mthread**. Define the class head with import packages and variable declarations. Multiple threads are detailed using printing at different intervals.

    ```
    public class mthread
    {
    ```

2. Define the head of the Java main method with declarations.

    ```
    public static void main(String args[ ])
    {
    ```

3. Define three task names.

    ```
    bprint task1, task2, task3;
    ```

4. Allocate three objects.

    ```
    task1 = new bprint ("task1");
    task2 = new bprint ("tsak2");
    task3 = new bprint ("task3");
    ```

5. Print a message that the threads are starting.

    ```
    System.out .println("\nStarting task threads");
    ```

6. Start three threads.

    ```
    task1.start ( );
    task2.start ( );
    task3.start ( );
    ```

7. Print a message that all threads are started.

    ```
    System.out.println("Threads for all task started\n");
    ```

8. Define the tail of the Java main method.

    ```
    }
    ```

9. Define the tail of the bthread class.

    ```
    }
    ```

10. Define the head of the bprint class with declarations and inherit Thread.

    ```
    class bprint extends Thread
    {
       private int sleepTime;
    ```

11. Define the head of the bprint class constructor.

    ```
    // bprint constructor assigns name to thread
    // by calling Thread constructor
    public bprint (String name)
    {
    ```

12. Set the thread name.

    ```
    super(name);
    ```

13. Define a random sleep time between 0 and 5 seconds.

    ```
    sleepTime = (int) (Math.random( ) * 5000);
    ```

14. Write the thread name and the sleep time on the console.

    ```
    System.out.println("Name: " + getName( ) + "; sleep: " +
               sleepTime);
    ```

15. Define the tail of the bprint class constructor.

    ```
    }
    ```

16. Define the head of a run ( ) method to execute the thread.

    ```
    public void run( )
    {
    ```

17. Define the head of a try block to put the thread to sleep for a random interval.

    ```
    try {
    ```

18. Print the thread name that is going to sleep.

    ```
    System.out.println(getName( ) + " going to sleep");
    ```

19. Sleep the thread with a time sleepTime.

    ```
    Thread.sleep(sleepTime);
    ```

20. Define the tail of the try block.

    ```
    }
    ```

21. Define the head of a catch block for an InterruptedException.

    ```
    catch (InterruptedException exception)
       {
    ```

22. Print a message when an InterruptedException occurs.

    ```
    System.out.println(exception.toString( ));
    ```

23. Define the tail of the catch block.

    ```
    }
    ```

24. Print the thread name that has completed sleeping.

    ```
    System.out.println(getName( ) + " done sleeping");
    ```

25. Define the tail of the run method.

    ```
    }
    ```

26. Define the tail of the bprint class.

    ```
    }
    ```

Implemented application using multiple threads that is saved in a file called **mthread.java**.

```java
// Show multiple threads printing at different intervals.
public class mthread
{
  public static void main(String args[ ])
  {
    bprint task1, task2, task3;

    task1 = new bprint ("task1");
    task2 = new bprint ("tsak2");
    task3 = new bprint ("task3");

    System.out .println("\nStarting task threads");

    task1.start ( );
    task2.start ( );
    task3.start ( );

    System.out.println("Threads for all task started\n");
  }
}

class bprint extends Thread
{
  private int sleepTime;

  // bprint constructor assigns name to thread
  // by calling Thread constructor
  public bprint (String name)
  {
    super(name);

    // sleep between 0 and 5 seconds
    sleepTime = (int) (Math.random( ) * 5000);

    System.out.println("Name: " + getName( ) + "; sleep: " +
                  sleepTime);
  }

  // execute the thread
  public void run( )
  {
    // put thread to sleep for a random interval
```

```
    try {
        System.out.println(getName( ) + " going to sleep");
        Thread.sleep(sleepTime);
        }
    catch (InterruptedException exception)
      {
        System.out.println(exception.toString( ));
      }
    // print thread name
    System.out.println(getName( ) + " done sleeping");
  }
}
```

Figure 55. Multiple Threads Printing

11.3. The Runnable Interface

In this section you need a way to inherit from multiple classes. To implement multiple classes you need to implement interfaces. Java provides the Runnable interface as an alternative to the Thread class. Create a clock called **bclock** that clicks after the initial display using the **JApplet** class. The clock should run and allow the user to browse other HTML code. In this case the Applet for the clock is places on a different thread. This is done with a Runnable interface in the Applet. An implementation guideline for the Runnable interface is:

Clock Code	Description
public class bclock extends JApplet implements Runnable	Add implements Runnable in the applet class declaration.
private Thread timer = null;	Declare a thread instance, timer, with the initial value null.

public void init( )
{ if (timer == null)
    { timer = new Thread(this);
      timer.start( );
	Create a new thread in the applet's init( ) method an start it.

public void start( ) { timer.resume( ); }	Resume the thread in the applet's start( ) method.

```
public void run( )                      The thread to execute the run( ) method.
{ while (true)
    { repaint ( );
      try {timer.sleep (1000); }
      catch (IOException e) { }
    }
}
public stop ( ) {timer.suspend ( ); }   Override the stop( ) method to suspend
                                        the running thread.

public destroy ( ) {timer.stop ( ); }   Override the destroy ( ) method to
                                        kill the thread.
```

The bclock applet uses a different technique than SimpleThread for providing the run method for its thread. Instead of subclassing Thread, bclock implements the Runnable interface that implements the run method. bclock then creates a thread and provides itself as an argument to the Thread's constructor. The Thread gets its run method from the object passed into the constructor. Figure 56 details an application for a threaded clock called **bclock**.

Steps that implement a GUI that implements Runnable threads are:

1. Implement a Java program that uses Thread in a GUI called **bclock**. Define the class head with import packages, inheritance, and variable declarations.

   ```
   import java.awt.Graphics;
   import java.util.*;
   import java.text.DateFormat;
   import java.applet.Applet;
   public class bclock extends Applet implements Runnable
   {
      private Thread clockThread = null;
   ```

2. Define the head of the start method.

   ```
   public void start( )
   {
   ```

3. If no clock thread exist create a clock thread and start the created thread.

    ```
    if (clockThread == null)
    {
       clockThread = new Thread(this, "Clock");
       clockThread.start( );
    ```

4. Define the tail of the start method.

    ```
    }
    ```

5. Define the tail of the start method.

    ```
    }
    ```

6. Define the head of the run ( ) method to execute the threads.

    ```
    public void run( )
    {
    ```

7. Allocate a thread object.

    ```
    Thread myThread = Thread.currentThread( );
    ```

8. Define the head of the while loop to compare threads.

    ```
    while (clockThread == myThread)
    {
    ```

9. Repaint the window.

    ```
    repaint( );
    ```

10. Define the head of the try block.

    ```
    try
    {
    ```

11. Set the sleep method to a time constant.

    ```
    Thread.sleep(1000);
    ```

12. Define the tail of the try block.

    ```
    }
    ```

13. Define the head of the catch block. Every try block must have a corresponding catch block.

    ```
    catch (InterruptedException e)
    {
    ```

14. Define the tail of the catch block.

    ```
    }
    ```

15. Define the tail of the while loop.

    ```
    }
    ```

16. Define the tail of the run method.

    ```
    }
    ```

17. Define the head of the paint method.

    ```
    public void paint(Graphics g)
    {
    ```

18. Get the time and convert it to a date.

    ```
    Calendar cal = Calendar.getInstance( );
    Date date = cal.getTime( );
    ```

19. Format the date and display it on the screen.

    ```
    DateFormat dateFormatter = DateFormat.getTimeInstance( );
    g.drawString(dateFormatter.format(date), 5, 10);
    ```

20. Define the tail of the paint method.

    ```
    }
    ```

21. Define the head of the stop ( ). Overrides Applet's stop method, not Thread's.

    ```
    public void stop( )
    {
    ```

22. Set the clockThread to null.

    ```
    clockThread = null;
    ```

23. Define the tail of the stop method.

    ```
    }
    ```

24. Define the tail of the bclock class.

    ```
    }
    ```

Implemented application that implements Runnable threads in an applet that is saved in a file called **bclock.java**.

```
// Threaded Clock example program
import java.awt.Graphics;
import java.util.*;
import java.text.DateFormat;
import java.applet.Applet;

public class bclock extends Applet implements Runnable
{
  private Thread clockThread = null;
  public void start ( )
  {
    if (clockThread == null)
    {
      clockThread = new Thread (this, "Clock");
      clockThread.start ( );
    }
  }

  public void run ( )
  {
    Thread myThread = Thread.currentThread ( );
    while (clockThread == myThread)
    {
      repaint ( );
      try
      {
        Thread.sleep (1000);
      }
```

```
      catch (InterruptedException e)
      {
        // the VM doesn't want us to sleep anymore,
        // so get back to work
      }
    }
  }

  public void paint (Graphics g)
  {
    // get the time and convert it to a date
    Calendar cal = Calendar.getInstance ( );
    Date date = cal.getTime ( );
    // format it and display it
    DateFormat dateFormatter = DateFormat.getTimeInstance ( );
    g.drawString (dateFormatter.format (date), 5, 10);
  }

  // overrides Applet's stop method, not Thread's
  public void stop ( )
  {
    clockThread = null;
  }
}
```

The HTML code is:

```
<html>
<applet code = "bclock.class" width = 350 height = 200> </applet>
</html>
```

Figure 56. Threaded Clock

The bclock applet's run method loops until the browser asks it to stop. In the iteration of the loop, the bclock repaints its display. The paint method figures out what time it is, formats it in a localized way, and displays it.

11.4. Synchronization

When more than one thread is running that are mutual exclusive the threads can execute from start to the finish of the processes. A way is needed to communicate and coordinate actions between threads. Threads make progress through their code at independent rates. This generates a need to coordinate threads. Consider the threads as workers in a factory with dependent production lines. At times one thread must wait until another thread has completed a number of statements before other threads can continue their execution. Coordination of concurrent activities is called **synchronization.**

A thread is blocked if its continued execution is delayed until a later time. One way to block a thread is the use of a timed loop to delay thread execution progress. For example, a loop with a shared **flag** variable to delay a thread is:

```
while (flag != true) {sleep (t);}
```

This delay is called a busy wait. Another way to delay a thread execution is to use the suspend ( ) method.

11.5. Exercises

1. Write an applet to display a flashing label.

2. Write an applet to display a moving label. The label moves from the right to the left continuously in the applet's viewing areas.

3. Write a program to launch 10 threads. Each thread is to add 1 to a variable sum. The variable sum is initially set to zero. You need to pass sum by reference to each thread. Define an integer wrapper object to hold sum. Run the program with and without synchronization to see its effect.

About the Author

Dr. Edward Hill, Jr. has been in the information profession since 1964. He has held technical and managerial positions in government including: Mathematician, Computer Systems Analyst, Survey Statistician, and Supervisory Survey Statistician from 1964–1996. He has worked as an Adjunct Associate Professor of Computer Science from 1978–1996 at Howard University. He has worked as an Associate Professor of Computer Science from 1996–present at Hampton University. He has been a Computer Science Consultant since 2000. Dr. Hill is a widely recognized expert in database design, computer information science, data resource management, and data-related planning, analysis, and design methods. He has taught many undergraduate and graduate courses in computer science and information management. Dr. Hill is distinguished by his ability to communicate concepts clearly, simply, and effectively to any audience detailing his experiences in computer science and other areas.

Dr. Hill is a graduate of Southern University (B.S. degree with major in mathematics/education), Atlanta University (M.S. degree with major in mathematics), and The George Washington University at Washington, DC (D.Sc. with major in Computer Science, minors in Applied Mathematics and Operations Research).

Index

abstract, 18, 83-84, 121, 140-142, 145, 169, 190, 199-201
abstract class, 83-84, 140-141
abstract method, 83-84, 141, 199-201
Abstract Windowing Toolkit (AWT), 145
AbstractButton, 176
ActionEvent, 152, 154-155, 169-170, 173, 175-176, 178-179
actionPerformed, 150, 152, 154-155, 173, 175, 178-179
actual parameters, 80, 116, 132
addMouseListener, 190, 192-193, 196
age_cal, 150-151, 153-156
age_cal.java, 153, 156
Applets, 113, 121, 146, 149-150, 157
appletviewer, 145, 149, 156
arithmetic operators, 7
array, 123-128, 132-136, 158-159, 161, 163, 211-212
array of objects, 125, 158-159
assignment statement, 6-7, 9, 19
Assignment Statement, 6-7, 9, 19
base case, 85-86
bclock, 219-220, 223-224
bclock.java, 223
board, 2, 98, 198, 200-201

board.java, 200
boolean, 1, 10-12, 20, 23-24, 29, 36, 42, 48, 140-141, 164, 203-204, 214
boolean type, 23
border, 202, 205-207
Border layouts, 205
border.java, 207
BufferedReader, 32, 38, 44, 51, 59, 67, 104
BufferedReader class, 97
button types, 176
ButtonHandler, 176-180
Buttons, 151, 157, 159, 161, 176, 191-192, 203-207, 211-212
byte, 13, 18, 20, 141
Calling a Method, 80
capacity ( ), 131
case statements, 43, 46
caserang, 43, 46, 48
caserang.java, 46
Casting Objects, 141
catch block, 92, 107-108, 217, 222
catching an exception, 90
char, 1, 18-19, 22, 96, 125
character data type, 22
charAt ( ), 131
Checkboxes, 180

229

checkme, 180-184
checkme.java, 183
claiming an exception, 90
class, 112
class JApplet, 146
class String, 128
classname, 113-114, 117
classname objectname, 113-114
combob, 185-189
combob.java, 188
Command-Line Parameters, 132
compareTo, 129
compile, 13, 117, 120, 156
compiling, 120
concrete classes, 140
constant, 7, 19-20, 154, 158, 221
constant variable, 19
constructor, 114
Container, 157
container layout manager, 201
Control statements, 10, 12
copy arrays, 126
create an array, 124-125, 128, 135
Creating a Method, 77
Data Fields, 83, 112-113
Declarations, 18
derived class, 137
destroy, 146, 148, 220
direct superclass, 137
Directories, 95, 97, 118, 120
directory, 95
distance, 25, 81-83
do loop body, 64

do loop syntax, 64-65
dorange, 67, 70, 72
dorange.java, 70
double, 1
doubleValue ( ), 142
elserang, 37-38, 40, 42
elserang.java, 40
escape codes, 22
event handler, 169
event listener, 169
Event programming, 169
EventListener, 169, 190
exception, 89
exception handler, 90
exception handling, 89-90
Execute, 10, 12-13
extends, 137, 140
extension, 1, 113, 149, 156
file, 95
FileDialog, 96-97
FileWriter, 106-108
final, 18, 20, 111, 140
finally block, 92-93
first_apple, 148-150
float, 1, 18, 20, 22, 130, 141
flow, 203
flow.java, 204
FlowLayout, 202-204
folder, 89, 95
for loop, 48-56, 59, 67, 125, 128
For loop, 48-56, 59, 67, 125, 128
for Statement, 11, 51
formal parameters, 79-80

forrang, 51, 53-56
forrang.java, 54
getButton ( ), 192
getFile ( ), 97
GridLayout, 207, 209-210
hexadecimal, 21-22
HTML, 145, 148-150, 156, 219, 224
ibuf, 100-104
identifier, 77-78, 154
identifiers, 17-18
if body, 29-30, 36
if else, 29, 36-38, 40-41, 54
if else Statement, 36-37
if else statements, 29, 40, 54
if head, 29-31, 36
if statement, 10, 29, 31, 36, 42
if statements, 29
if-else statements, 37, 40
ifrange, 32, 34, 36
ifrange.java, 34
import, 120
import statement, 111, 120-121, 146
inf, 101-104
Inheritance, 137
init, 146, 148-154, 203-204, 206-207, 219
initializer list, 125
input stream, 96, 101, 103
insert ( ), 131
Instance methods, 113, 117, 137-138
Instance variables, 113-114, 116, 137-138, 149
int, 1, 20

iobuf, 100-101, 103-104
iobuf.java, 103
ItemEvent, 169, 180, 182, 184, 186, 188
ItemEvents, 185
iteration, 12, 48, 72, 85-86, 224
java, 13
Java, 111
Java applet, 145
Java exception model, 90
Java standard class library, 140, 201
Java Swing GUI Components package, 145
java.io package, 96
java.lang package, 89, 140, 214
javac, 13, 120, 156
javax.swing, 100, 103, 120, 145-146, 148-151, 153, 156-157, 165, 167, 169-171, 173, 176, 178, 180, 183, 185, 188, 193, 195, 198, 200, 203-204, 206-208, 210
JButton, 146, 159, 176-180, 208-210
JCheckBox, 146, 180-183
JComboBox, 146, 185-186, 188
JOptionPane, 102, 104, 150, 152, 154, 157, 160-161, 164-165, 173, 175, 178-179, 182, 184-186, 188, 199-201
JOptionPane class, 157
JPasswordFields, 170
JTextFields, 170
Keyboard, 2-4, 25-27, 32-35, 38-41, 44-48, 51-55, 59-64, 67-72, 96-99, 146, 170, 198
Keyboard Input, 2-4, 34, 38, 40, 44, 46, 51, 54, 59-60, 62, 67, 70, 96-99
keyin, 98-100

keyin.java, 99
keyPressed ( ), 198
keyReleased ( ), 198
keyTyped ( ), 198
keyword supper, 139
label, 42-43, 150-151, 153-154, 159, 165-168, 176, 186-189, 196, 225
Label, 42-43, 150-151, 153-154, 159, 165-168, 176, 186-189, 196, 225
label.java, 167
launch, 213
layout manager, 201
length, 6, 13, 15, 17, 74, 109, 122, 124-126, 129-134, 143, 150, 161, 209-210
length ( ), 131
literal, 20, 22, 128
Load mode, 96
location, 6, 116, 120, 123, 126, 129-131, 190
long, 18, 20, 141, 214
loop body, 48, 64, 86
method, 77
method body, 77-78, 116
Method Syntax, 78
Methods, 1
modifiers, 77, 115, 140, 193
Modifiers, 77, 115, 140, 193
mouseClicked, 191, 194, 196
MouseEvent, 169, 190-192, 194-197
MouseListener, 169, 190, 192-196
MouseMotionListener, 169, 190-193, 195
mthread, 215, 218

mthread.java, 218
multidimensional array, 126
multiple-dimensional array, 128
multithreading, 213
myfirst.java, 1, 4, 13
Numeric wrapper classes, 141-142
numeric wrapper object, 142
Numerical Data Types, 20
object, 112-113
Object class, 140, 142
Object-oriented programming, 111, 143
octal, 21-22
Open, 1, 10, 93, 96-97, 109
Operator Precedence, 23-24
operators for Boolean, 23
option (-d), 120
output stream, 96, 106, 108
Overloading, 81, 111
Overloading Methods, 81
package, 117
package names, 121
paint, 146, 148-149, 157, 222, 224
pan, 208-211
pan.java, 210
Panel, 160, 202-203, 205-211
parameter, 79-80, 104, 116, 118, 126, 139, 158-159
Parameters, 77-80, 86, 116, 132, 139, 155, 158
parseInt ( ), 142
Pass by Value, 80
Passing Parameters, 80
Polymorphism, 137

position number, 123, 125-126
precisions, 20
pressme, 176-180
pressme.java, 178
Primitive type data, 130
println, 117
Private methods, 78
Program comments, 24
Program Comments, 24
public method, 77, 140
quadratic.java, 113, 119-120
ratio method, 91
Recursion, 85-86
recursive call, 85
recursive step, 85
reserved words, 17-18, 20
return, 79
return type, 77-79
reverse ( ), 131
run ( ), 214
Runnable interface, 219-220
Save mode, 96-97
scope of a variable, 117
scope of the loop, 11
secondary storage devices, 95
select range, 31, 37, 43, 51, 59, 67
short, 18, 20, 141
shortcut form, 42
shortcut operators, 21
Shortcut Operators, 21
simple Java model program, 1
Single-thread programs, 213
start, 146

start ( ), 214
stop, 25, 73, 146, 148, 214, 220, 222-224
stop ( ), 214
String, 128-129
String Comparisons, 129
String Concatenation, 129
String variable, 97, 129
StringBuffer, 130-131
StringBuffer class, 130-131
StringTokenizer class, 131
subscripted arrays, 128
Substrings, 130
super, 139
superclass constructor, 84, 138-139
Superclasses, 138-139, 157
suspend ( ), 214
switch expression, 42-43
switch label, 42
Switch statement, 42-43
synchronization, 224-225
syntax of a for statement, 11
syntax of a while, 12
Textfield, 151-155, 174-175, 205
textpass, 170-175
textpass.java, 173
tfo, 106, 108
tfo.java, 108
this, 139
thread, 158, 213-225
Throwable class, 89-90
throwing an exception, 90
throws clause, 77-78
toString ( ), 142

tracker, 193-197

tracker.java, 195

Translate, 13

travel, 82-83

try block, 92, 107-108, 217, 221-222

type casting, 21-22

types of exceptions, 89

Unicode, 17, 22

Using Packages, 120, 122

valueOf, 142

variable, 6

Variables, 18

Web browser, 145

While loop, 56

while Statement, 12, 59

wrange, 59, 62, 64

wrange.java, 62

wrap int to Integer, 141

978-0-595-35422-1
0-595-35422-X

www.ingramcontent.com/pod-product-compliance
Lightning Source LLC
Chambersburg PA
CBHW051230050326
40689CB00007B/867